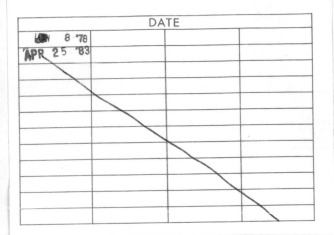

DATE		
JUN 8 '78		
APR 25 '83		

Hawaiian Americans

AN ACCOUNT OF THE MINGLING OF JAPANESE, CHINESE, POLYNESIAN, AND AMERICAN CULTURES

BY

EDWIN G. BURROWS

ARCHON BOOKS
1970

ISBN: 0-208-00949-3
Library of Congress Catalog Card Number: 73-122394
Printed in the United States of America

Contents

HAWAIIAN AMERICANS

I

One Question Leads to Another

O N Sunday morning, December 7, 1941, when
Japanese planes swooped on Pearl Harbor, residents of Hawaii of Japanese descent numbered
about 160,000. That was more than a third of the total
population; more than the total in Hawaii of any other
one ancestral stock; and more than the total of Japanese
ancestry in all the continental United States. To be sure,
less than a quarter of the 160,000 had been born in Japan,
and these—the men among them—were well past fighting
age. But the Hawaiian born, the nisei, numbered nearly
125,000. They were all young, and included about 25,000
males between the ages of 18 and 38—the makings of a
formidable military force.

Even their legal citizenship was in doubt. Japan
claimed the older ones by virtue of their Japanese parentage, the United States by virtue of their birth on American
soil. As a gesture of good will Japan had in 1924 relin-
quished claim on those born after that date and provided
a way for those born earlier to expatriate from Japan.
But how many had done this before Pearl Harbor seems
to be uncertain. Certainly a great many had not and remained "dual citizens."

During the years of recurrent tension between the
United States and Japan, probably all Americans who
knew about these nisei had wondered how they would
act in case of war between the country of their ancestry

and that of their own birth. Pearl Harbor put that question to the test. Bits of the answer had wide publicity during the war in newspapers and magazines—particularly War Department press releases and articles by Blake Clark listed in the bibliography. Through them the outstanding military record of Hawaii's nisei soldiers became widely known. More recently Dr. Andrew W. Lind of the University of Hawaii has given an admirably full answer in his book *Hawaii's Japanese: an Experiment in Democracy*. He presents some unquestionable examples of adherence to Japan and many of confused and apparently wavering behavior.* But many more, seemingly far the greatest number, proved themselves loyal to the United States. (Illustrations of the extremes of this range of response will be given in later chapters of this book.) Lind sums up: "Out of the travail of war, born of the heroic sacrifice of thousands of Hawaii's best youth on the battlefields of the world and the fearful pain of greater thousands of their parents and kin throughout Hawaii, there has emerged a devotion of spirit to American values and ideals such as the Islands have never before witnessed."

This answer raises another question: "How did so many people of Japanese parentage become American in one

---

* Undecided allegiance is hard to detect in overt behavior. It was expressed clearly, though, in a poem written by one of the nisei while interned in Hawaii because of suspicion as to his loyalty. A censor's translation of the poem, which was written in Japanese, follows:

> Morning and evening we salute the flag at the top of the pole.
> The wordless silvery-clear sound of the bugle imitates for
>   mankind the call of destiny.
> Our military spirit wavers between Yasukuni and this place.

Yasukuni is the shrine in Tokyo dedicated to those who have died for the Emperor.

generation?" But answering that requires, first of all, asking still another question. For Americans and Japanese are not the only peoples represented in Hawaii. The influences that shaped the nisei were the result of a process that had been going on long before Japanese immigrants —except for a few castaways on derelict sampans—ever reached Hawaii. So our question must take a broader form: How have the different peoples in Hawaii affected each other?

In one way that is a little *too* broad. We are not interested, here, in changes of physique as a result of interbreeding. So our question is, more precisely: How have the different cultures represented in Hawaii affected each other?

"Culture" is used here in the anthropological sense, to mean behavior shared by learning, as distinguished from behavior biologically inherited. Culture in this sense includes customs, language, arts and crafts, institutions, intellectual assumptions, sentiments, standards, interests, insofar as these are passed about as traditional or customary. Thus a culture comprises a vast number of patterns for living, which all compose one great pattern. That is what we have in mind, though vaguely as a rule, when we use such a phrase as "the American way of life." Ordinarily the people living at one time in one region all conform to the same pattern in the main, although any culture permits more or less individual variation.

To go back to the beginning, ever since human beings came down out of the trees and began to walk about on two feet, they have been given to wandering over the face of the earth. As means of transportation improved, they migrated farther and in greater numbers. In the last few centuries, with the development of large ships and navigation in European culture, groups from widely separated areas with correspondingly wide differences in culture have been brought together in many places. The result is an interchange of cultures, which American anthropologists call acculturation.

Hawaii is one of the places where this process has gone farthest. These islands were among the last habitable spots on earth to be settled by man. The first human beings to reach them were Polynesians from similar islands in the tropical Pacific. Nobody knows when the Polynesians aboard some double canoe first caught sight of the clouds hanging over the blue peaks of Hawaii. All we need to know here is that Polynesians, called Hawaiians from now on, were first on the ground by centuries; and that they developed out of their traditional lore a culture which supported a numerous population and gave answers to most of their problems.

Next came Europeans and their kinsmen, Americans of European descent. The Hawaiians called them haole.* The word has been adopted in the English spoken in the islands and will be used here as less cumbrous than "Euro-American." Now the culture of the haoles, as will appear in detail later, included equipment and procedures which gave them a decided advantage over the Hawaiians in many respects. The time came when haoles had control of a good deal of the best land. Their plans for using it required more labor than they could perform themselves. And the Hawaiians, for reasons which will also come up later, were not steady workers.

* In English, the pronunciation "howly" is near enough.

The haoles went to the ends of the earth in search of hands to work their plantations. One of the most satisfactory early sources of supply was the Canton delta of China. Imported plantation hands, though, were not the first Chinese to reach Hawaii. As early as 1789 a few Chinese taken on at Macao by the schooner *Eleanor* are said to have left the ship to settle in the islands. Others, mostly merchants, came in, a few at a time, throughout the first half of the nineteenth century. But all such immigration was in small numbers compared to the importation of plantation hands. That began in 1852 when two shiploads, numbering about 300 in all, were brought in by the Royal Hawaiian Agricultural Society.

At first Hawaii seems to have liked the Chinese better than some of them liked Hawaii; for Prince Liholiho reported to the Society in 1864 that "with all their faults and a considerable disposition to hang themselves they have been found very useful." But as soon as the Chinese had served their time in the cane fields, many of them moved into town and opened little shops. At this they were so successful that during the 1880's haole merchants and artisans objected vociferously to the competition. Immigration was restricted in 1883 and stopped altogether in 1886. Yet haole planters still wanted more field hands. The royal cabinet investigated the issue. Their report, issued in 1889, sums up as follows: "The excessive proportion of Chinese in the kingdom, and their rapid encroachment upon the various businesses and employments of the country, require adequate measures to prevent the speedy extinction in these Islands of western civilization by that of the East, and the substitution of a Chinese for the Hawaiian and other population." Immigration was resumed in 1893, but only for a few years. Ever since the peak of immigration around 1880, the population of Chinese descent has ranged from 20,000 to nearly 30,000; enough to give Chinese, or more precisely Cantonese, culture substantial representation in the life of the islands.

The first importation of laborers from Japan was in 1868.* Like the Chinese, they had been preceded by a few of their fellow countrymen. Early Japanese arrivals were mostly fishermen whose sampans had been blown off their course, and who had managed to survive until the currents took them to Hawaii. Japanese arrivals of this kind may well go back to pre-European times. But they were so few that they never formed a distinct element in the population.

Dissatisfaction in Japan with the way the first Japanese contingent had been recruited and shipped to Hawaii, and with the way the men were treated after they arrived, halted further immigration from this source until 1884. But once immigration from Japan got well under way it outstripped all others. From 1885 to 1899, arrivals from Japan numbered 65,045. And a larger proportion of Japanese than of Chinese stayed on in Hawaii.

During the 1890's, and particularly after the Hawaiian monarchy was succeeded in 1893 by a provisional government, the influx of Japanese aroused fear and opposition, as the Chinese had done a decade earlier. The competition that was feared this time was not so much economic as political. The provisional government was pointed toward annexation of Hawaii by the United States. The rapidly

* The fullest source on this subject is *A History of the Japanese People in Hawaii* by Ernest K. Wakukawa (Honolulu, 1938).

increasing numbers of Japanese, and some of their actions and those of their home government, gave rise to suspicion that Japan was trying to take Hawaii away from the United States. How much truth there may have been to this is not clear. At any rate, it gave another shove toward annexation, which was accomplished in 1898.

In 1907 Japanese immigration was curtailed by the "gentleman's agreement" between Japan and the United States. But a supplementary arrangement, which some wag called the "ladies' agreement," provided for admission of brides for Japanese bachelors already on American soil. From then until the immigration was ended by the Immigration Act of 1924 (often called the Japanese Exclusion Act), Japanese immigration consisted largely of "picture brides," so called because bride and groom were frequently introduced to each other by a convenient haole device, the photograph. By 1900 the Japanese had become the most numerous ethnic group in the population of Hawaii and remained so until after Pearl Harbor.

These are by no means the only sources of immigration to Hawaii. Another large early importation was that of Portuguese from Madeira and the Azores. The latest, and eventually next to largest, was from the Philippines. Smaller groups came from various parts of the South Pacific, from Korea, Puerto Rico, Spain, Germany, a few from still other places. Study of these peoples could test and supplement the conclusions reached here. But in order to get an answer to our general question, which will at the same time answer the specific one about the American nisei, study of four of the cultures represented in Hawaii—Hawaiian, haole, Chinese, Japanese—seems enough. In fact, if a personal confession is admissible, study of four cultures seems enough for any one life-time. Probably nobody ever attains an exhaustive knowledge of one culture. Many a time during more than three years spent on this inquiry from about 1930 on, I vowed never again to undertake a problem that involved driving cultures four-in-hand!

Now that the question is clearly in mind, the next point is how to go about finding an answer. Several methods were tried successively. The one that seemed to get farthest was to look at the matter from the point of view of an individual brought up in twentieth-century Hawaii. Such an individual—for example, a nisei, member of a Japanese family, in an American territory, inhabited also by Hawaiians, Chinese, and various other peoples—grows up in the presence of several different cultures. He has to choose among different ways of living; in detail, among different ways of doing almost everything. Most of his choices may not be deliberately thought out. He may be quite unaware of a great many of them. But he has to make them just the same.

Now any choice, any preference for one course over another, is determined by one or more values. In this sense a value is simply any attribute regarded as desirable.* So our protean question about how the nisei in Hawaii became American at last takes final form: What values have governed the run of choice among cultures in Hawaii?

An example will illustrate what is meant by a value and how values work in this situation. One of the pro-

---

* G. A. deLaguna in *Speech: Its Function and Development*, defines a value as an "objectified affect." This is essentially the same concept, except that here only positive or pleasant affects are included.

cedures attempted during early stages of this inquiry was
to compare the rates of change among different practices.
Without going into the evidence, it seemed that diet (or
food habits in general), language, and religion changed
more slowly from Hawaiian or Oriental toward American than most other practices did. That brought up the
question, what have these three activities in common to
make people more conservative about them than about
other matters? The concept of choice governed by values
had not been formulated at that time. I would now phrase
the question in this way: What values favor choice of old
or ancestral ways of eating, talking, and worshiping?

This question was put to members of the Anthropological Society of Hawaii at a meeting in which I presented a tentative report on the subject of this book.
Pearl Beaglehole suggested an answer: "Early condition-
ing." In other words, people learn ancestral ways of eating, talking, and worshiping earlier and more thoroughly
than they learn ways of doing most other things. So
these particular ways are more deeply ingrained and less
readily changed. The value that governs choice in such
cases I call familiarity, for lack of a better name; though
the word is hardly strong enough.

Obviously this is not the only value involved in choice
among different languages, religions, or food practices.
Language is probably the most complex of cultural patterns, hence the hardest to learn. So another value retarding acquisition of a new language would be economy
of effort. Again, religion has a value all its own: the se-
renity born of assurance that there is a power strong
enough to solve all problems, dispel all dangers. Many
of the religious beliefs other than Christian that seem par-

ticularly tenacious in Hawaii are concerned with agriculture, fishing, and healing. Now neither haole science nor
haole religion offers a sure way to get a good crop, a
good catch of fish, or recovery from disease. Anxiety
about such matters is more readily relieved by rituals
that we call "magic" and "superstition," than by relying
solely on haole techniques, which promise no more than
to reduce the likelihood of failure.

Another center of tenacious old beliefs is sorcery. Both
haole science and haole religion do deny that any such
practices are effective. But this does not seem enough to
overcome the fear of them. A Hawaiian student at the
Kamehameha School for Boys in Honolulu, when asked
by the principal whether he believed in such dark forces,
said, "No, I don't believe in them. Still, there's no use
taking a chance." So the value of relief from anxiety,
even more than that of familiarity, retards abandonment
of old religious or magical beliefs.

Food habits seem to be the purest case of the value of
familiarity as a brake on change. Everyone has noticed
in our culture how many people only enjoy dishes to
which they have long been accustomed. Whoever has to
plan a dinner for a considerable number of people—as
long as it is not a society of gourmets—knows that it is
safest to be guided by a standard bill of fare. That is
why distinguished foreign visitors to the United States,
in peacetime at least, get so tired of beefsteak and roast
chicken.

This illustration not only makes clear what is meant by
values governing choice among cultures, and how such
values are inferred from prevalent behavior, but also
shows the hopelessness of trying to identify all the values

at work in so complicated a process as acculturation in Hawaii. They vary so, according to individual characteristics and particular situations, that they are innumerable. Nevertheless, since Hawaii, per acre of land or head of population, must be one of the most voluminously written-up places on earth; and since the people there are friendly, and willing to answer even rather impertinent questions, it seemed possible, with patience, to make out some of the main values that have governed the progressive choice of American culture there. That is what the following pages try to do. The answer must include not only how haole culture became dominant in the first place but also how the stress imposed on other peoples by that dominance was relieved without disrupting the society; and finally, how the conclusions drawn from study of Hawaii may help toward understanding, and perhaps improving, similar situations elsewhere.

Publication of this study is made possible through a grant from the Viking Fund. During its preparation, office room was granted by the Bishop Museum and by the Honolulu Council of the Institute of Pacific Relations, for about a year each, and by the University of Hawaii for several months. The staffs of all these institutions were generous with time and counsel. Professor Felix M. Keesing, then at the University of Hawaii, kindly allowed use of papers contributed by students in his anthropology classes, and of material gleaned by Henry Silverthorne from the Archives of Hawaii. A discussion of the subject before the Anthropological Society of Hawaii yielded several valuable suggestions. Any attempt to list the social scientists who have read the manuscript, or parts of it, and made suggestions would seem like gilding the result with great names. Fundamental information came from so many residents of Hawaii that it is impossible even to remember, let alone thank them all. The greatest obligation is to my wife, who stood by during those lean years.

PART 1

THE GROWTH OF HAOLE PRESTIGE

II

The Growth of Haole Prestige among Hawaiians

THE Hawaiians' first glimpse of haole culture must have been a ship. Probably the first ships were Captain Cook's *Resolution* and *Discovery*, which anchored off the island of Kauai in 1778.* How the natives felt, on seeing these tall square-riggers against the sky, is suggested in a Hawaiian account translated by Fornander: "One said to another 'What is that great thing with branches?' Others said 'It is a forest that has slid down into the sea,' and the gabble and noise was great. Then the chiefs ordered some natives to go out in a canoe and examine well that wonderful thing." Another hint of the early impression made by foreign ships is the fact that the word for them in Hawaiian is not *wa'a*, the name for their own canoes, but *moku*, which means "island."

Wonders did not cease when the Hawaiians came aboard Captain Cook's ships. For that we have Cook's own word:

In the course of my several voyages, I never before met with natives of any place so much astonished, as these people were upon entering a ship. Their eyes were continually flying from object to object; the wildness of their looks and gestures fully expressing their entire ignorance of everything they saw. And it does their sensibility no little credit, without

* E. W. Dahlgren, *Were the Hawaiians Visited by the Spaniards before Their Discovery by Captain Cook in 1778?* Dahlgren's answer is "No."

flattering ourselves, that when they saw the various articles of European manufacture, they could not help expressing their surprise, by a mixture of joy and concern, that seemed to apply the case as a lesson in humility to themselves; and on all occasions they appeared deeply impressed with a consciousness of their own inferiority.

Several values are suggested by these accounts. One may be called show. The Hawaiians were apparently struck with admiration by the sheer bulk, complexity, and glitter of the strangers' equipment. This instance is also one of several suggesting that Polynesians are particularly susceptible to another value, that of novelty. The Hawaiians' dazzled first impression is poles apart from those recorded of various other primitive peoples, parties of whom have visited modern European or American cities and remained quite blind to the display of engineering virtuosity all about them. In such cases, apparently, the new sights are too far out of their experience to mean much to them. But the Hawaiians, expert boatbuilders and seamen themselves, were well able to appreciate the advantages of Captain Cook's capacious and seaworthy craft, and of much of his other equipment.

Surprisingly, they recognized iron, and showed their visitors a few pieces of it that they already had. Yet there is no iron ore in Hawaii worth working. Besides, the mining and smelting of iron ore were unknown anywhere in Polynesia. What little iron these Hawaiians had may have drifted to Kauai on some derelict sampan or bit of wreckage from Japan.* The people of Kauai al-

---

* This point is argued convincingly by John F. G. Stokes, *Iron with the Early Hawaiians*, Hawaiian Historical Society Papers, No. 18 (Honolulu, 1936).

ready knew by experience that the newcomers' cutlery was better for hewing wood than the ground stone tools that were all their culture had. They prized iron so much that they were inclined to go overboard with any loose bit of it they could lay hands on. In other words, they saw in the strangers' equipment not only show and novelty but also the solider value, utility.

One more value is suggested by Captain Cook's statement that the wonders of his ships and ships' gear awoke in the Hawaiians a feeling of inferiority. They seem to have made the generalization that because the foreigners were superior to them in certain points of technology, they were superior in everything. Now generalization is a process as universal among human beings as language. Indeed, language itself—the Hawaiian as much as any other—is built out of generalizations. Yet the human job of generalizing, as the preachers of semantics keep on telling us, is rarely well done. Science is essentially a careful way of generalizing; and generalizations made even in that august name can be very bad. No wonder, then, that the Hawaiians, accustomed to accepting mysteries and miracles as part of their daily lives, readily took a general haole superiority on faith. This acknowledgment of general superiority, beyond reach of any test, constitutes the powerful value of prestige. Its power, of course, does not depend upon whether the judgment of superiority is justified or not; only on the strength of the conviction. In Hawaii haole prestige became the master value that to a great extent governed the course of history.

When Captain Cook reached the island of Hawaii and anchored at Kealakekua Bay, the natives were at first completely overwhelmed. Here was a rare case of prestige at first sight. They went so far as to take Captain Cook for their god Lono. They escorted him and his shore party to one of their sacred enclosures and made him the offerings due to divinity. The fair skins of the strangers probably had something to do with it. Among themselves fair skin was valued as a sign of nobility. Within any one race, those who sit in the shade and receive tribute are lighter-hued than those who have to work for a living out in the sun. Besides, Lono was supposed to be a fair-skinned god. The fact that the skins of the newcomers were fairer than the fairest in the Hawaiian range of complexions, added to the splendor of their ships and trappings, made the conclusion that Cook was Lono fairly plausible.

Faith waned however as the visitors put a strain on the food supply, gave other intimations of mortality, and gradually wore out their welcome. When the two ships, after once setting sail, put back to await a more favorable wind, the Hawaiians were anything but glad to see them back. No danger of Captain Cook being worshiped this time. There were quarrels and reprisals, and the final proof of Cook's mortality was given by a Hawaiian wooden dagger that took his life.

It was only at Kealakekua that haole prestige burst like a skyrocket into sudden glory and then went out almost as suddenly. Elsewhere it grew slowly. Just how slowly, varied locally according to the amount and nature of experience with haoles. It varied individually, too, according to a variety of experiences and predispositions that affected the impression the strangers made. Some Hawaiians eagerly welcomed the new ways; others resisted. The values involved in this range of individual difference could only be made out by detailed life histories. They cannot even be listed here. Enough instances are on record, though, to show the widespread effect of the values already mentioned, and a few others.

The continuing strength of show and novelty is illustrated by the eagerness of Hawaiians, in the early days, to get from their visitors a variety of wares for which they had no practical use. For instance, Freycinet saw at Kealakekua in 1819 a store of glittering compasses, sextants, thermometers, and clocks. There is no evidence that anybody there at that time knew how to use them. But the clearest illustration of the values of show and novelty is the eagerness of the chiefs, who alone among Hawaiians could afford such luxuries at first, for foreign clothing. Surely their own scanty wraps were better suited to the mild climate of Hawaii than haole sheaths and casings, designed to shut out the cold of higher latitudes. Yet in spite of utility the Hawaiians craved the gorgeous new raiment. Among many descriptions, that of Kotzebue, which dates from 1816, is one of the most vivid:

My guests had all dressed themselves in their best attire. I scarcely recognized Kareimoku, who shone in the dress of an English pilot, with polished boots, and a cocked hat; but all his things were so tight, that he could scarcely move a limb, and the noon-day's heat threatened to stifle him in his costume. Not less proud, but equally distressed, the other jerries [*ali'i*, chiefs] moved in their European dresses; and we saw here sailors, coxcombs, and Moravians, confusedly mixed together. The Americans certainly buy up in their cities all the clothes which are out of fashion, and sell them here to great advantage.

Self-preservation, which commonly outweighs all other values in a pinch, is strictly speaking an extreme form of utility. Yet it is a special case; a negative one, since the acts it motivates are acts of avoidance or defense. So it has proved convenient here to label it as a separate value. Self-preservation was of the greatest importance in the development of haole prestige in Hawaii. Nothing drove home the conviction of haole superiority quite so inescapably as powder and ball.

One first impression of the strangers' weapons is pictured in Captain Nathaniel Portlock's account of his visit to Waikiki in 1786. He was warned that the chief there, Kahekili, intended to attack him, presumably to get possession of the ship and its contents. Kahekili had heard of firearms but never seen them in action. Portlock says:

After being on board some time, he was very desirous to see the effects of our firearms, which I showed him, by discharging a pistol loaded with ball at a hog that stood at some distance, and killed it on the spot. The king and his attendants were startled at the report of the pistol; but when they saw the hog lie dead, and the blood running from the wound, they were both surprised and terrified; and I have not the least doubt but this instance of the fatal effects of our firearms made a deep impression on their feelings, and prevented them from attacking us.

Other chiefs were less prudent, and other foreigners gave their demonstrations with human targets. Early contacts were as often fights as frolics. The first instance was at Kealakekua when the natives were fired upon, and Captain Cook himself was killed. In spite of the gravity of the haoles' loss, the score in number of casualties

favored them. Four chiefs and 25 native commoners
were killed. In the considerable number of fights, mas-
sacres, and reprisals recorded in histories of Hawaii, the
showing was the same. Painfully the Hawaiians learned
respect for haole weapons. Captain Golovnin reported,
after his visit in 1818: "In the opinion of Americans, the
natives had to a great extent lost their warlike spirit and
bravery. Convinced of the superiority of firearms . . .
they neglected their own weapons."

Long before this, though, a number of the chiefs had
converted the negative value of self-preservation into the
positive value of utility, by making use of haole weapons
in wars among themselves. As early as 1792 Captain James
Vancouver was horrified by the apparent depopulation
of the islands since his visit, 14 years earlier, as one of
Captain Cook's officers. He attributed the change to in-
cessant warfare among the chiefs. On his return voyage
he could hardly get provisions except in exchange for
arms and ammunition. "Their great avidity for procur-
ing these destructive engines," he wrote, "may possibly
have been increased by the successes of Tianna who, it
should seem, is principally indebted for his present exal-
tation to the firearms he imported from China, and those
he has since procured from the different traders. His example has produced in every chief of consequence an
inordinate thirst for power, and a spirit of ambition seems
generally diffused amongst them."

Only one of the chiefs, in the long run, could make
this kind of ambition come true. That one was Kamehameha, from the island of Hawaii; a chief of high rank,
yet not first in line of succession on that island. He is the
most conspicuous example of the strength of the value of

utility in stimulating adoption of haole devices. In his campaigns against rival chiefs he used not only haole fire-arms but haole ships. Archibald Campbell, about 1809, counted more than 30 in the royal fleet. By that time Kamehameha's shrewd use of haole implements had helped him to extend his rule over the whole Hawaiian archipelago, something that none of his predecessors had ever achieved.

Wherever Kamehameha saw an advantage in haole technology, he made use of it. Captain John Turnbull noted in 1802; "He has European and American artificers about him of every description." Lisiansky, two years later, put their number at more than 50. Nor did he confine himself to material goods. Probably one of his greatest aids along the road to power was the counsel of two haole mariners, Isaac Davis and John Young, captives at first, who reconciled themselves to finishing their lives in the royal service.

Yet this shrewd chief held fast to the value of utility. He would take nothing on faith. True, he indulged, like other chiefs, in haole clothing, and that of the gaudiest. But in his case this seems to have been mainly for the purpose of making a dignified appearance before haoles. For comfort, he sensibly preferred the native loincloth; and for regal state before his own people, continued to wear his famous yellow feather cloak. He also had a good deal of European household equipment. Golovnin listed among his effects (1818) a set of silver tableware, ground-glass dishes, two tables, two or three chairs, a bottle of rum with some glasses, a large mahogany bureau, and a mirror. This too (except for the rum, which his advisers had to warn him to beware of) he reserved mainly for entertaining and perhaps impressing foreign guests.

When it came to diet and table manners, Kamehameha kept, somewhat defiantly, to Hawaiian ways. Kotzebue, after describing the dinner served in more or less European style to his party, goes on:

He made an apology for eating in our presence, and said "I have seen how the Russians eat; now you may satisfy your curiosity and see how Tamaahmaah (Kamehameha) eats." The table was not set out, but the dinner was ready placed in a distant corner, on banana leaves, which served instead of dishes . . . The repast consisted of boiled fish, yams, taro roots, and a roasted bird, a little larger than a sparrow, which lives on the summits of the mountains. It is very rare, and is a dish only for the royal table. . . . Instead of bread, he ate the taro-dough, which when diluted with water, becomes a soft pap; and though the king possesses very handsome table utensils, it stands in a gourdshell at his right hand, in which he dips his forefinger when he eats fish or flesh, and dextrously stuffs a good portion of it in his mouth; and this slovenly way of eating is observed from the king down to the least menial. Tamaahmaah, who, during the whole repast, had made use only of his fingers, perceived very well that I attentively observed his motions, and said to me, "This is the custom in my country, and I will not depart from it."

This little scene unmistakably suggests that Kamehameha felt himself under pressure to acknowledge haole prestige, but was deliberately resisting.

Kamahameha similarly refused to accept haole religion. This choice was presumably motivated not only by familiarity, as in the case of diet and table matters, but also by utility. For a man of his intelligence could not fail to see how the native Hawaiian religion, with its sacred tabus and its attribution of divinity to chiefs, reinforced his own power. Kamehameha died before an organized Christian mission reached Hawaii. But an attempt was made to convert him by a man who, according to Vancouver, had formerly been a clergyman in England. Captain Richard Cleveland describes this attempt:

Among others at this early period was a Mr. Howell, commonly called Padre Howell, who soon ingratiated himself into favor with the King, and, being struck with the superiority of his intellect, conceived that it would not be difficult to induce him to abandon his idolatrous worship and substitute one of rationality. Accordingly he lost no opportunity, after acquiring a sufficient knowledge of the language, to convince the chief of the incapacity for good or evil of his gods, and of the power, wisdom and goodness of the Supreme Maker and Ruler of the Universe, whom he worshipped. The first, that of impotency of the idols, was without difficulty admitted; but the second, not being tangible, could not be comprehended. His mind, however, appeared to be dwelling on the subject with increased attention after each conversation. At length, one day, while walking together, the King unusually thoughtful, and Howell auguring favorably from it, the silence was broken by the King's observing: "You say your God is powerful, wise, good, and that he will shield from harm those who truly worship and adore him." This being assented to, then said the King: "Give me proof, by going and throwing yourself from yonder precipice, and while falling, call on your God to shield you, and if you can escape unharmed, I will then embrace the worship of your God." It may be unnecessary to say that Howell failed to give the desired test, and that the king remained unconverted.

This story had a long time to grow in the retelling before Cleveland reached the islands; yet it fits what we know of Kamehameha, and may well be substantially true.

Enough has been said of Kamehameha to show that he was an exceptional person. Certainly he was exceptional in his hardheaded picking and choosing from haole culture. Most Hawaiians seem to have let the big and little values offered by foreign wares and ways accumulate in their minds until the generalization of haole prestige grew upon them unawares. Though no explicit statement of such a conclusion has been found, instances of Hawaiian behavior tell it more clearly than words.

To continue with the example of religion, the native faith was perceptibly weakened by foreign influence before Christian missionaries arrived. Presumably the main reason was the doubt awakened by foreigners when they ignored Hawaiian tabus, yet did not suffer divine wrath in consequence. Women, particularly hampered by tabus, were ready skeptics. Archibald Campbell, a mariner who stayed on Oahu longer than most foreigners in the years just before the advent of the mission, and has left the best account of that period, concluded his discussion of the recurrent tabu periods with this comment:

Notwithstanding the rigor with which these ceremonies are generally observed, the women very seldom scruple to break them, when it can be done in secret; they often swim off to ships at night, during the taboo, and I have known them eat of the forbidden delicacies of pork and sharks' flesh. What would be the consequence of a discovery I know not, but I once saw the queen transgressing in this respect, and was strictly enjoined to secrecy, as she said it was as much as her life was worth.

One value behind this choice of haole freedom from tabu was, of course, enjoyment of the good things to eat. Such choices also involved the more general value of release from irksome traditional restrictions. This might be called a form of utility. But again it seems useful not to stretch that term too far, but to give specific names to particular forms of it that seem to have been important.

Loss of faith in the native Hawaiian religion had gone far by 1817, when Kotzebue, admitted to a sacred enclosure in Honolulu, found the priests themselves irreverent. After describing the grotesque wooden images, and the offerings left to rot before them, he says: "Though the smell was to me very disagreeable and the sight of the idols laughable, I did not let the islanders perceive it, that I might not offend them; but I was the more astonished when the priests themselves made me observe the caricatures, felt their noses and eyes, tried to imitate, in various ways, the distorted faces, and laughed heartily at their wit."

One step further along this way brought some Hawaiians to the point of adopting the haole religion, even without tangible proof of its superiority to their former faith. A choice like that comes very close to acceptance of haole prestige. Captain Freycinet records the baptism of two Hawaiian chiefs, Kalaimoku and his brother Boki, by the chaplain of his ship in 1819. One of them even told him that their mother had died a Christian. She may well have been the first Hawaiian convert.

Whichever was the first, certainly the most notable early conversion was that of Opukahaia ("Henry

Obookiah"), one of many young Hawaiians who shipped during those years on foreign vessels, especially whalers. He reached New Haven, Connecticut, in 1809, took an intense interest in haole ways, and made friends who took a corresponding interest in him. The story that he was found weeping on the steps of one of the Yale college buildings, because haole enlightenment was denied to his people, became for at least a generation a favorite among evangelists. Opukahaia died in 1818 at Cornwall, Connecticut, where he was preparing for mission work among the Hawaiians. His example did much to rally the first band of missionaries, which sailed from New Haven in 1819 and reached Hawaii, by way of Cape Horn, in the following year.

Meanwhile Kamehameha, staunch bulwark of the old religion, had joined his divine ancestors. His son and successor Liholiho, who was far from being a chip off the old block, had been persuaded by two of the royal widows, Keopuolani and Kaahumanu, to abolish the system of tabus which gave religious sanction to most of the prevalent restrictions on conduct. Liholiho announced this change by publicly eating with women, in violation of one of the strictest tabus. He is said to have fortified himself for this venture by a potion of haole liquor. The breaking of tabus was followed by the burning of wooden images of the gods. Thus the missionaries found the way to some extent prepared for them.

The story of their struggles and achievements has been told time and again. Toward their main goal, substitution of Christianity for the native religion, they made rapid progress, in outward forms at least. The public, institutional side of native religion disappeared rapidly.

Native holy days and religious assemblages went out of use. Priests lost official status. Most of the wooden images were burned. Mourning customs objectionable to the mission, such as knocking out teeth and scarring the body in token of grief, disappeared. Infanticide was at least driven under cover. In 1824 the high chieftess Kapiolani defied the dread goddess of volcanoes, Pele, by going in chiefly state to the brink of the active crater at Kilauea, ignoring the homage supposed to be required by Pele, and challenging the goddess to punish her.

Still the change was not as complete as these incidents might suggest. In 1824, the same year in which Kapiolani defied Pele, Reverend Asa Thurston of the pioneer missionary band wrote: "Though this people have cast away the greater part of their idols . . . so far from renouncing their belief in the former Gods of Hawaii, it is supposed that more than two-thirds adhere to them in some measure, and sacrifice unto them in private." Survivals and revivals of native religion will be brought out in more detail later.

Nevertheless, there is no reason to question the depth and sincerity of many Hawaiian conversions to Christianity. If the converts differed from their teachers in interpretation of the new faith, so did their teachers differ from other Christians even in their own native New England. If intensity of feeling is taken as the test, there is evidence of that even to the point of violent bodily disturbance. Hiram Bingham, a moralist rather than a mystic, reported of an evangelistic service on Kauai in 1832: "One of the persons who rose, a man of perhaps 50 years . . . appeared to be seized with a sort of convulsive agitation or involuntary shaking, of his whole body, head, and limbs, as he stood, though he seemed unable to stand—a man who stood by clasped his arms around his body, and sat down with him upon a form, holding him with considerable strength while he continued to shake less and less for about 10 minutes." If quiet and steady service is a better measure of religion, the history of the mission in Hawaii contains many instances of lifelong devotion to Christian work among Hawaiians. Individual cases could be cited, ranging all the way from this extreme to the opposite. If all the evidence could be assembled and evaluated, Hawaiian Christianity might come off fairly well in comparison with that of any other country. With their own traditional faith lost, or at least shaken, Hawaiians found in Christianity the unique value that any sincere religion gives—and it was one they badly needed—the assurance that in spite of all hazards they would be taken care of, and everything would come out right.

In attempting to change Hawaiian ways in matters not strictly religious, missionary success varied widely. Much depended upon whether haole influence was united in favor of a particular change, or whether haoles not of the mission opposed it. Putting clothes on the Hawaiians is an example of missionary success, where the mission had help from a variety of sources. We have noted a taste for European finery among the chiefs in premissionary times, and how traders were glad to gratify it, at a profit. The Englishman George Beckley, when put in command of the fort at Honolulu, had advanced the cause further by introducing a uniform in European style for his garrison. His insistence that the men keep it on won him the nickname *Humehume* (cover up). Still another ally of the mission in this campaign was the mosquito, introduced in the water casks of a whaler about 1827. With all these adventitious aids, it is no wonder that the missionaries' sermons and sewing circles put more and more native skin out of sight.

But covering their bodies did not mean that Hawaiians had adopted Christian standards of chastity. Here the mission had to fight the extracultural value of sexual gratification, which every culture has trouble in keeping within bounds. It also had to fight the lust of nonmissionary visitors to Hawaii, who were all male in those days. Their appetite for Hawaiian women was whetted by the enforced celibacy of a long voyage; and unchecked, in these remote islands, by the restraints of home. Moreover, the way was cleared for them by a certain freedom or laxity in Hawaiian custom. Hawaiian culture had, to be sure, its own strict rules regulating marriage. Except where sacred rank was involved, Hawaiians went further than haoles in prohibiting marriage between relatives. Yet when it came to preserving the purity of a noble strain, they went even further with inbreeding than European royalty did; encouraging in some cases marriage between brother and sister of the highest lineage. But chastity, of itself, was not valued in their culture. A number of unrestrained love affairs was part of the experience expected of young people before marriage. After marriage, liaisons could be arranged by consent of all concerned. Mourning ceremonies for a high chief ended in an orgy of sexual license. Two of the native games (*ume, kilu*) involved sexual relations. And Hawaiian hospitality might go the length of lending a woman to a guest. This privilege seems to have been extended rather generally to foreign sailors on shore leave.

The meeting of these two standards of sexual morality —that of the Hawaiians and that of the sailors—led to calling nearly all rules off while a ship was in port. By 1792, when Vancouver revisited Hawaii, he noted the prevalence of open solicitation by and for Hawaiian women. On his first visit, with Captain Cook, he had seen nothing of the kind. In 1820, the mission's first year in the islands, the Mission Journal reported: "To the stranger, who enters their habitations of ignorance and depravity, the husband offers his wife, the father his daughter, and the brother his sister! When solemnly assured, there is a God in heaven who forbids and abhors such iniquity, they reply: 'Other white men tell us it is right; but you are strange white men.' "

When the missionaries attempted to deprive visiting sailors of what they had come to regard as a vested right, the sailors objected violently. In 1825 Reverend William Richards was virtually besieged in his house at Lahaina, Maui, by a crew of frustrated and furious fellow Americans. In the same year, and for the same reason, Reverend Hiram Bingham was in danger of his life for a time in Honolulu.

While the conflict soon passed this violent stage, the mission never did win out, except with individual converts. This point could be established in some detail.* In order to keep it from bulking out of proportion, it will be supported here only by two bits of evidence. In 1846 Chester Lyman reported a conversation with the missionary Reverend W. D. Alexander:

* See for example H. B. Restarick, *Hawaii, 1778–1920, from the Viewpoint of a Bishop* (Honolulu, 1924).

Mr. A's opinion is that licentiousness in the Islands, and especially in the ports, can hardly be said to be on the decrease—rather the contrary . . . Hundreds of [or?] thousands of girls, the finest in the kingdom, come to Lahaina and Honolulu from all parts of the Islands solely for the purpose of prostitution. . . . The public officers are as vigilant as possible, and do all in their power to prevent them from going on board ships or coming in contact with sailors. But in many cases it is said husbands and parents connive at this wickedness, letting out for money their own wives and daughters. Many of the foreign residents here are of the most corrupt class, and act as pimps for seamen and sea captains.

In the second half of the nineteenth century Iwilei, near Honolulu Harbor, became one of the notorious brothel districts of the Pacific. Hawaiians were no more involved now than other elements of a variegated population. Still later, when this district was "cleaned up," the problem remained; but by this time had pretty well got out of the hands of both Hawaiians and missionaries.

Missionary failure could be demonstrated in some other respects, where the mission was similarly opposed by worldly haoles. The mission did not succeed in suppressing the Hawaiian dance (hula); indeed, it was the more erotic forms of the dance that survived best under missionary ban, due to haole demand for them as a naughty spectacle. Nor could the mission prevent the spread of some haole practices to which it objected; notably the drinking of alcoholic liquor and the smoking of tobacco. On these points, too, many witnesses could be cited.

But these missionary defeats were still, in the main, haole victories. They did not retard the growth of haole prestige. The citations just given show how even the traffic in women gradually took on the haole pattern of commercial prostitution. And in matters where the missionaries were unopposed, they had a great deal to do with gradually making over Hawaiian life to conform to a haole model.

As powerful as the church was another agency of theirs, the school. When the government finally took over the school system, the New England plan on which the mission had established it was retained, and the missionary Richard Armstrong became the first Minister of Education. A glimpse of how deeply this influence penetrated is given by accounts of old Hawaiian myths, written down by Hawaiians who had been trained in mission schools. Samuel Kamakau, in his version of a Hawaiian creation myth, has the first woman made out of the rib of a man. Kepelino divides his ostensibly native creation story into six days, and calls the seventh "the tabu day of Kane." * Abraham Fornander, pioneer collector of Hawaiian folklore, found the native "major pantheon" interpreted as a trinity: "I learn that the ancient Hawaiians at one time believed in and worshipped one God, comprising three beings, and respectively called Kane, Ku, and Lono, equal in nature but distinct in attributes." This scheme relegated Kanaloa, fourth of the major pantheon, to the role of "a fallen angel, antagonistic to the great gods, and the spirit of evil and death in the world." Fornander, in his eagerness to trace the Polynesians back to the Arabian Peninsula, accepted this version as ancient and authentic. But data now available from other parts of Polynesia support the obvious con-

* One of the gods; pronounced "Káh-neh."

clusion that this is another case of reinterpretation under missionary influence. Transformation of old myths, hallowed by tradition and endeared by familiarity, shows how missionary influence disturbed the depths of the converts' thoughts and feelings.

After the first 20 years or so, both missionary effort and Hawaiian zeal for the mission perceptibly relaxed. This change has been established so clearly by Blackman, in his pioneer study *The Making of Hawaii*, that it need not be reargued here. But the loss in haole influence from this source was more than made up by a gain from other haole sources, especially those working for commercial and political advantages.

Attempts to develop Hawaii commercially begun even before the arrival of the mission. Most of the beginnings were feeble. One, the shipment of sandalwood to Canton, where it was in great demand for making incense, grew so fast that it disturbed Hawaiian life seriously for a time. But it did not last long. The chiefs exploited this source of quick wealth so enthusiastically that about 1830 the supply of the fragrant wood gave out. The only remnant of this trade now is the Cantonese name for Hawaii, which means "Sandalwood Mountains."

Political encroachment had begun even earlier. Kamehameha I made a kind of cession of the island of Hawaii to Vancouver, as representative of Great Britain, in 1794.* In 1815–16 a German physician, Dr. Georg Scheffer, acting on behalf of Russia, made what seems to have been a fumbling attempt to set up a Russian outpost in the

---

* For a fuller account of the events sketched in here, see Ralph S. Kuykendall, *The Hawaiian Kingdom, 1778–1854* (University of Hawaii, Honolulu, 1938).

islands; but when Kamehameha ordered him off, he did not feel strong enough to resist. One of the great events of the reign of Kamehameha II was a visit to England; the last event, too, for he died in London in 1824. The high chief Boki seems to have told King George IV, just after Kamehameha's death, that the king had intended to acknowledge the British crown as his overlord. In a note to King George on this subject, Secretary Canning said that "the Governments both of Russia and of the United States of America are known to have their Eyes upon those Islands." The relationship between Hawaii and Britain in those days amounted to something like a discreet, informal protectorate.

During the 1830's Kamehameha III was harassed by a whole series of threats to his sovereignty, instigated mainly by the consuls of the two strongest European powers, Britain and France. It looked as if these men— Richard Charlton for Britain, Jules Dudoit for France —were deliberately stirring up trouble, with a view to intervention and perhaps occupation by their respective countries. Feeling ill equipped to handle such difficulties, the king and chiefs in 1836 asked the American Board of Commissioners for Foreign Missions to find them a teacher in political science, interpreter, and adviser. The Board recommended a man already in the islands, William Richards, who resigned from the mission in 1838 and spent the rest of his life in the service of the Hawaiian monarchy.

One of Richards' first acts in his new capacity was to write to William Butler, attorney general of the United States, asking for a treaty between the two countries. "I have been the more ready to make this request," his letter says, "from an apprehension entertained by many that some of the governments may yet seize on these islands for their own advantage. A formal treaty between this government and the United States, would tend to prevent such an attempt, and thus not only secure in some degree the welfare of this people, but also to prevent future difficulties between the United States and England or Russia, the nations most likely to take possession of these islands."

The fears of the Hawaiian rulers were well justified, although the first to move was not England or Russia but France. In 1839, in response to a complaint from Dudoit about the expulsion of French Catholic missionaries, Captain Laplace arrived with the frigate *Artémise*. Under her guns the king not only granted the establishment of a Catholic mission, but also made concessions to French trade, particularly importation of wines and brandy, which the American mission had opposed. In 1843 the British took their turn, backing up the flimsy complaints of their man Charlton. The frigate *Carysfort* descended on Hawaii. Her commander, Captain Lord George Paulet, raised the Union Jack over Honolulu and put a British commission in charge. Some of those who talk about Hawaii in the sunny vein that seems to be induced by the climate have made much of the point that the islands were never conquered. But here was a bloodless conquest. And it was bloodless only because the Hawaiians were too well aware of the superiority of haole arms to risk a fight. To be sure, when the matter came before Paulet's home government in London, his highhanded act was disowned. But the prestige it cost the Hawaiian monarchy could not be given back. Again self-preservation contributed mightily to haole prestige.

American naval vessels called, too, on similar errands: in 1826 the *Peacock*, Capt. Thomas ap Catesby Jones; in 1829 the *Vincennes*, Capt. William C. B. Finch; in 1832 the *Potomac*, Capt. John Downes; in 1836 the *Peacock* again, with Commodore Edmund P. Kennedy aboard. The most persistent issue was the claim of American traders for payment of debts incurred by the chiefs during the sandalwood boom. There was no overt aggression by the Americans. Yet Captain Jones, in a letter to the king, submitted claims which the United States "has the will, as well as the power to enforce, when other, and more pacific measures are disregarded." And Commodore Kennedy is said to have assumed a "very imperious" manner. The Hawaiian rulers knew perfectly well that these were fighting ships.

In 1849 the French came again, with two warships under Admiral de Tromelin. They took possession of Hawaiian Government buildings and destroyed property, but did not attempt to annex the islands permanently. In 1854 rumors reached Hawaii that a filibustering expedition was being organized in California to seize the islands. The king had had enough. He opened negotiations for annexation by the United States. But he died before the year was out, and his annexation project died with him.

The new king had no intention of yielding his sovereignty. Besides, among foreign powers he seems to have favored Britain rather than the United States. Indeed, the "lavender-scented" court of this king, Kamehameha IV, and his successors, illustrated haole prestige by imitating, as far as possible, all the trappings of European royalty. In 1866 (the king then was Kamehameha V) the scene impressed the youthful Mark Twain, though not in the way intended. He wrote:

And let it be borne in mind that there is a strictly defined "court costume" of so "stunning" a nature that it would make the clown in a circus look tame and commonplace by comparison; and each Hawaiian official dignitary has a gorgeous, vari-colored, gold-laced uniform peculiar to his office —no two are alike, and it is hard to tell which is the "loudest." The king had a "drawing room" there at stated intervals, like other monarchs, and when these varied uniforms congregate there weak-eyed people have to contemplate the spectacle through smoked glasses.

So even when they tried to blazon forth their own power and glory, these later Hawaiian kings took a haole way of doing it. The imitation did not stop at outward show, but included the form of government. The king had his ministers and his Parliament. Still more indicative of the dependent state into which the monarchy had fallen is the fact that when the sovereignty of Kamehameha III was threatened by haoles, it was to other haoles that he had to look for help. Under these circumstances, haole prestige could hardly be resisted any longer, unless by some of the humbler Hawaiians who, in out-of-the-way valleys, kept on living in much the old way. Even the mission had changed them only a little.

At length haole encroachment began to reach out even to the farthest corners of the land. During these middle years of the nineteenth century peaceful infiltration was more continuous than open aggression, and in the long run more successful. Some of it, as in the case of the mis-

sionaries who turned statesmen to help the monarchy out
of its troubles, came from the best of motives. Some of it
was sheer greed. Either way, it was taking leadership
away from the Hawaiians; and this in economic as well
as political concerns. Some haole commercial undertakings beside retail trade in the seaports, were now beginning to take hold. Cattle ranching was the first endur-
ing success. Rice growing, introduced by the Chinese,
was the most important of many agricultural ventures as
long as the island economy was largely self-contained.
It was a Chinese, too, who began the commercial cultivation of sugar cane, of which the Hawaiians used to raise
a few stalks in their gardens even in pre-European days.
But this industry, which was to dominate the economic
life of Hawaii later on, was developed mainly by haoles.
With them, too, it grew slowly at first. Yet on the whole,
haole agriculture kept on growing.

All these enterprises took land.* Foreigners were acquiring more and more of the best of it, and in Hawaii
the supply is limited. Grants of land to foreigners had
begun in the time of Kamehameha I, but for a long time
were regarded, according to old custom, as subject to
the pleasure of the ruling chief. But as haoles began to
make a success of using the land, they wanted to make
their holdings permanent. In this they were supported
by some Hawaiian cultivators; for the more progressive
of these complained that they had little inducement to
make improvements, if the only result was to be to catch

* The history of land tenure in Hawaii has been told, more fully
than would be relevant here, by Dr. Andrew W. Lind in *An Island
Community* and by Jean Hobbs in *A Pageant of the Soil*. Dr. Lind's
book is a study of ecological succession. That of Miss Hobbs is partly
a defense of missionaries against persistent charges of land grabbing.

the eye of a greedy chief, who would promptly take over.

During the 1840's an effort was made, with the help of the less mercenary of the whites themselves, to stem the tide of acquisition by foreigners. An act passed in 1845 prohibited aliens from acquiring fee simple title to land. In 1848 the whole system of land tenure was revolutionized by the "Great Mahele," a division of all land in the kingdom into four classes. Land of one class went to the king; of another to the government; of a third to the chiefs; and the rest to the tenants.

Though one of the motives of this change was to help Hawaiian commoners, it had the opposite effect, when followed in 1850 by abolition of the law preventing foreigners from acquiring land. From then on, the commercially naïve Hawaiians were besieged by foreigners with offers to buy; or else, with the joys of ready cash in view, tried of their own accord to raise money on their land. Accustomed to interdependence among kinsfolk, and to looking to their chiefs for help, they were slow to grasp the finality of these new transactions, and the individual responsibility involved in them. When Hawaiians got money by selling or mortgaging their land—proceedings which few of them understood—their inclination was to share their new wealth freely, according to old custom, with relatives, friends, or chance comers. After the money was all gone, they looked to their kinsfolk, or to their chiefs, for help. But kinsfolk and friends were apt to be as poor as themselves, unless they had adopted the haole policy of every man for himself. And the chiefs had lost the power to redistribute land.

The outcome is summarized in a passage from the diary

of Reverend Amos Starr Cooke, written in June, 1851, the month when he left the mission to become one of the founders of the firm Castle & Cooke, later the biggest of the "Big Five" which dominated business in Hawaii.

It seems as if Providence was fighting against the nation internally. . . . Diseases are fast numbering the people with the dead and many more are slow to take advantage of the times and of the privileges granted to them by the King and Government. . . . While the natives stand confounded and amazed at their privileges and doubting the truth of the changes in their behalf, the foreigners are creeping in among them, getting their largest and best lands, water privileges, building lots, etc., etc. The Lord seems to be allowing such things to take place that the Islands may gradually pass into other hands. This is trying but we cannot help it. It is what we have been contending against for years, but the Lord is showing us that His thoughts are not our thoughts, neither are His ways our ways. The will of the Lord be done.

The sugar industry, retarded for decades by lack of an assured market, came into a fortune with the passage, in 1875, of a Reciprocity Treaty with the United States. Hawaiian sugar was admitted into the United States duty free, in return for use of Pearl Harbor as a United States naval base. With that godsend, Hawaiian sugar rapidly grew into Big Business, and Hawaii became one of the most prosperous areas anywhere in the tropics.

But Hawaiians of the native race lost rather than gained by this prosperity. The business of promoting, developing, and managing sugar plantations was quite beyond them. Their abilities had been developed in other directions. They were not even a success as plantation laborers, in spite of their physical stoutness. The whole idea of steady work for wages was so foreign to their old culture that it had no value to appeal to them. As for work, most of that in their old life came in short bursts, spaced out by stretches of leisure. They enjoyed the bursts of work, which were also social gatherings, and gave scope for display of physical prowess. They enjoyed, even more, long intervals of sociable idleness. Spending the whole day in the cane fields was not only disagreeable, but, to their way of thinking, an inexcusable waste of time. They could see no sense in helping to produce inordinate quantities of sugar cane when they did not get the sugar, and could not have used it if they had.

Money, of course, was supposed to make steady work worth while. But that meant very little to the Hawaiians. True, they could see—all too clearly—the advantages of ready cash. But the idea of saving it up for the distant future was almost wholly lost on them. They had always got along without putting by "for a rainy day," as the haoles call it. Food was, to them, about the most important form of material wealth; and their kinds of food, with few exceptions, would not keep. Land, the source of much of their food, was not exchanged for other goods in their old culture; and, as we have seen, they did not fully grasp the haole system of trading in land until it was too late. If a Hawaiian did accumulate a surplus of material goods, he was promptly besieged by relatives and friends—"calabash relatives," the haoles call those not closely related by blood, because the sharing of food is so important in the relationship. These joyfully helped the prosperous Hawaiian get rid of his surplus. He could not turn them off. According to his upbringing, the way for a man to enhance his status through material wealth was not to store it up but to give it away with lavish generosity.

The result of all this was that when a Hawaiian was hired to work on the plantations, he would work, as a rule, only until he had enough money to buy what he wanted at the moment, and to give his friends a good time. No use showing up for work again until what he had was gone. The same background prevented Hawaiians from fitting into other niches in the new economy. As a consequence, Orientals were brought in to work the plantations. Inured to steady work and thrift, they got along only too well to suit the humbler haoles, with whom they came into competition.

Through most of the nineteenth century Hawaiians still had their monarchy to take pride in. But at length even that was taken away from them. The overthrow of the monarchy, followed by a short-lived republic and then by annexation to the United States, was in part an outgrowth of haole economic dominance; but that is not the whole story. For example, Julius Pratt, in *Expansionists of 1898,* has emphasized the part played in it by the wave of imperialism that swept the United States during those years. Still another factor was anxiety to head off Japan, which had developed a suspicious enthusiasm for filling up the islands with her nationals. Japan even went so far as to protest against restrictions on this immigration by sending warships. Without attempting an adequate analysis, it seems fair to say this much: that the change was a haole movement, and that Hawaiians, in the main, submitted only because they could not help it.

The crisis—when the abdication of Queen Liliuokalani was demanded in 1896—brought into play again the old threat of haole weapons. There was a flurry of arming on both sides. The only recorded casualty is the gunshot wound of a Hawaiian policeman who tried to stop a wagon train ladened with arms and ammunition for the revolutionists. The greatest display of force was a landing party from the U.S.S. *Boston:* 154 sailors and marines, with 10 officers. In addition to their rifles they brought two light cannon. Their avowed aim was only to maintain order, and they never aimed their guns. Yet the royalists plainly counted them among the enemy. In her statement of abdication under protest, Liliuokalani said she was yielding "to the superior force of the United States of America, whose minister plenipotentiary . . . has caused United States troops to be landed at Honolulu, and declared that he would support the said Provisional Government." With annexation to the United States at the turn of the century the Hawaiians became members of a haole nation. Once more self-preservation had reinforced haole prestige.

In the economic structure that developed along with these political changes, a few haoles took up the room at the top. Oriental tradesmen and craftsmen, with other immigrants and less prosperous haoles, pretty well filled up the middle. Most of the Hawaiians were left at the bottom.

The Hawaiians have never regained a satisfactory economic position. At the time of annexation they had at least a virtual monopoly of commercial fishing; but within a few years the market was captured by better-equipped and better-organized Japanese fishermen. A number of recent comparisons, using such indices as bank accounts and applications for employment relief, show

Hawaiians to be the least prosperous of the major ethnic groups in the islands. A few of them still make a subsistence on the land. But paternalistic government attempts at resettlement, while they cannot be called outright failures, have had at most a very limited success.*

More and more, Hawaiians have drifted to the cities, especially Honolulu, where they make a meager living at jobs like stevedoring and truck driving, that most others are quite willing to leave to them. Many have only odd jobs of unskilled labor. Some, as sellers of *leis* (flower garlands), or as "beach boys," whose main function is instruction in surf riding or, after dark, singing to the accompaniment of steel guitar and ukulele, purvey to tourists what little is left in Hawaii of Polynesian romance.

Politically the Hawaiians have been much better off. By the terms of the Organic Act which made Hawaii a territory of the United States, all Hawaiians were admitted to full citizenship. Their tradition fitted them much better for American politics than for American business. The change from dependence upon chiefs to dependence upon political bosses was not too sweeping. Hawaiians soon became adept at trading political services, particularly votes and electioneering, for political favors, particularly jobs. Their economic plight has been relieved somewhat by government employment as policemen, firemen, park keepers, janitors in public buildings, and laborers on public works. They have had their share of more important and remunerative political positions.

---

* These attempts have been analyzed by Felix M. Keesing in *Hawaiian Homesteading on Molokai* (University of Hawaii, Honolulu, 1936).

A number of them have made a very good showing as government officials.

To this day an appeal to the Hawaiian vote is an essential part of any political campaign. Candidates often make speeches in Hawaiian as well as English. They appear at campaign rallies smothered in leis, and commonly bring with them troupes of Hawaiian singers and hula dancers. At least once, in the early days of territorial government, there was an attempt to make a racial bloc of the Hawaiian vote. The slogan was *Nana ka hili* (look at the skin). In those days the great majority of the electorate was dark skinned. If they had voted on that basis, the haoles would have been crowded out of office. Haole politicians, in alarm, quickly went to work in inner party councils, and persuaded both parties that the better policy was to appeal to all races by having all represented on the party tickets, and voting by party instead of by race. Doubtless most disinterested observers would agree that this was an instance in which their advice, selfish though it might be, accorded with wise public policy. They succeeded then, and the same line has been followed ever since, so that voting by race has never become characteristic of Hawaiian politics. Yet now that the Hawaiian born of Oriental stock have come of age by the thousands—particularly those of Japanese descent, who far outnumber the Hawaiians—the political importance of Hawaiians as a group is waning rapidly.

From the lowly position to which most Hawaiians have been reduced, haole prestige looms bigger than ever. Ernest Beaglehole, in *Some Modern Hawaiians*, sums up the situation: "All the Hawaiians with whom I have discussed the matter have agreed that Hawaiians do not fol-

low easily leaders from their own cultural group. . . .
All the Hawaiians were similarly agreed upon the fact
that Hawaiians best follow the lead of whites. . . . Historical experience since the first European contact has
directed the Hawaiian to look to the powerful newcomer
for leadership. . . . The Hawaiian has thus become accustomed to habits of dependence upon the white man."

III

The Growth of Haole Prestige among Oriental Immigrants

BY the time the Oriental immigrants reached Hawaii, that is, the bulk of them, imported for plantation labor during the latter half of the nineteenth century, haole prestige was decidedly in the ascendant. Moreover, a few circumstances may have inclined the newcomers themselves to swallow haole prestige whole. For one thing, they took orders at first from haoles, got their living from them, and so might have been expected to look up to them. For another, these immigrants had been selected out of their home populations by willingness to strike out along new paths. It took that willingness to make them leave home and come all the way to Hawaii. So they might have been expected to adopt new customs more readily than most Orientals.

On the other hand, several influences pulled the opposite way. The immigrants were in Hawaii only as transients, or thought they were. Their subordination to haoles was provisional, for a purpose of their own—to save money and take it back home. Signing up as contract laborers by no means meant acceptance of haole prestige in advance. Moreover, as time went on, the rough treatment many of them got turned them against their bosses. The introductory account of their immigration contains indications of that, and more will be given later. Finally, both Chinese and Japanese were fortified against change by a traditional esteem of their own culture which was as complacent as that of the haoles themselves. How far haole prestige penetrated among the immigrants under these circumstances is the next question to consider. The Chinese will be discussed first, then the Japanese. Some of the points noted for each singly apply as well to the other.

Those who carried out the intention to take their savings back to the old country proved thereby that haole prestige had not prevailed with them. But this inquiry, directed at changes in Hawaii, is concerned chiefly with those who settled there. Even of these, a good many stayed on only because they had to. They grew too old to work, without having managed to save enough to pay their passage home, or at any rate to support them there. About 1917 the number of aged Chinese beggars on the streets of Honolulu called public attention to their plight. The territorial legislature, the Hawaiian Sugar Planters' Association, and some of the Chinese societies joined in providing a home for them, which opened its doors in 1920.

In 1937 about 140 old Chinese were living at this home, up in Palolo Valley, and about 300 more, elsewhere about Honolulu, were receiving support from the Social Service Bureau. Miss Nell Findley, then director of the bureau, took a special interest in them, and got to know them about as well as anyone could without learning their several dialects. She reported no evidence of haole prestige among them—quite the contrary. Theirs was the exaggerated patriotism of the exile. China was to them the lost Paradise, where all was as it should be. An illustration of this is the fact that the only fight about the Sino-Japanese War on the books of the Honolulu police department in 1939 was not between a Chinese and a Japanese, but between two inmates of the Chinese old men's home. One radical among them ventured the opinion that China's management of the war was not all it might have been. Another resented this as sacrilege; resented it so furiously that the police had to be called in.

A feeling that immigrants who died in Hawaii were still in exile is shown by such acts as that of the Lung Doo Chung Sung Society, which in 1933 appropriated $2,000 to have about 500 bodies disinterred and shipped to China for reburial.

There remains a considerable proportion of the immigrants who settled in Hawaii by choice. These were the successful rice farmers, craftsmen, or merchants, who found themselves able to get along better in Hawaii than they could have done in China. Their advancement in the new country shows how ready they were to take advantage of any device, new or old, that was recommended to them by the value of utility.

Acceptance of haole prestige, of course, is another matter. In many respects even these successfully transplanted immigrants carried on, in Hawaii, a Chinese way of living. Rice cultivation, on which most of the rural immigrants depended for a living, was itself an importation of Chinese culture. Another, prevalent in the suburbs, was vegetable gardening, carried on with Chinese tools and by Chinese methods. In ways like these the value of utility preserved Chinese practices.

In the cities and towns, where outwardly more concessions were made to haole ways, another value, that of familiarity, is especially evident as a preservative of

Chinese culture. There the Chinese huddled together in little Chinatowns, where propinquity helped to preserve familiar Chinese ways. Familiarity shows, for instance, in retention by the Chinese of the partnership, a favorite form of business organization in China. Paul Goo found that in 1935, out of 336 partnerships that filed tax returns on the island of Oahu, 154 or 45 per cent were Chinese; a proportion far greater than that of Chinese in the population, or Chinese firms among the total of business enterprises. It was utility, though, that induced some of the immigrants to take advantage of the swarming of Chinese by opening restaurants, drug stores, groceries, and shops of various kinds to supply the ready local market for Chinese wares.

Familiarity united with other values (of which more later) to revive in Hawaii that profusion of societies, based on almost any common interest, which is characteristic of Chinese life. The nature of some of these, as brought out in a survey of them made by Chock Lun in 1935, shows that the value of familiarity was one of the motives behind them. Of a total of 47 in Honolulu, 16 were "Hui ken," whose members all came from the same district of the Canton delta in China. One advantage of such societies was that all members spoke the same dialect. This bond also united in another society about 1,000 of the Hakka, whose ancestors had come from the north several centuries ago into the Canton delta. The Hakka remained to some extent strangers there, differing in dialect and custom, and not intermarrying, as a rule, with the old Cantonese.

Utility figured in the formation of these societies, too, for all were agencies for mutual aid. Nine of them were occupational, that is to say, primarily utilitarian. They, too, preserved a pattern of the old culture, being much like the Chinese guilds.

There were so few women among the immigrants that the Chinese family can hardly be counted among importations to Hawaii. Yet the solidarity among kinsfolk which is so powerful in China was preserved in Hawaii in several ways. One way was, again, the formation of societies united by this bond. Five of the societies were composed of fellow clansmen, and another perpetuated a traditional alliance among four clans. Another way, followed by a great many immigrants, was to keep up allegiance to relatives and ancestors in China. In 1887, just after the high tide of Chinese immigration, Reverend H. H. Gowen wrote: "The Chinese are . . . very tenacious of old customs, and so devoted to their parents in China that they would die rather than grieve them. This strong parental love is at present one of the greatest obstacles to the extension of Christianity that we have." How well that loyalty outlasted the years was shown as late as 1935 by a student in one of Professor F. M. Keesing's anthropology classes, who wrote (using the technical term "sib" for the Chinese clan or "greater family"): "Every month my father sends money back to his mother in China for the maintenance of the sib relatives and for upkeep of the sib's property and land. When my brother had a son, he had to send money back to China so that there would be a simple ceremony for recognition of his son as a member of the sib."

Chinese religion comforted many of the immigrants during the early days of hardship and humiliation, and still comforts their declining years. The earliest instance

I find recorded, which dates back to within a few years of the first importation of field hands, shows its protective function all the more clearly for being a rather naïve instance of what would be called magic rather than religion by those who insist on a distinction between the two. S. S. Hill heard the tale from a planter named Pitman. Pitman came upon one of his Chinese employees melting down silver. Suspecting a counterfeiting scheme, he asked the man what he was up to. The Chinese explained that he was making silver bullets to shoot a devil "with whom he had already had several encounters, and in one of which he had lost his cue." He said he had tried leaden bullets with some effect, but was confident that silver ones would do the work.

Most of the Chinese societies included in their quarters an altar room. Of a number of Chinese temples in Honolulu, one, the Kwan Yin Temple now on Vineyard Street, was begun during the 1880's. Rice planters built little shrines in their fields. Coulter and Chun found one of these still in use during the 1930's. Reverend Frank Damon, during his tour among the Chinese in 1882, noted: "In many of the houses we saw large pictures of their favorite god, with joss-sticks sometimes standing near." Ancestral shrines were set up in the homes as soon as the immigrants acquired homes of their own.

The version of Chinese religion brought with the immigrants to Hawaii was not united into one institution. Each little temple was independent, sharing with the others only a common tradition. And this tradition encouraged, by precedent, continual foundation of new temples because of revelations to individuals. At least two temples in Honolulu, both named after the fisherman's god How Wong, were founded by immigrant minor prophets. The woman who founded the How Wong Temple on Fort Street was famous during her lifetime for saintly life and miraculous powers.

The younger and humbler founder of the How Wong Temple on School Street told Miss Sau Chun Wong his story (*Social Process in Hawaii*, 1937). He came from China as a boy and attended St. Louis College until the seventh grade, when he had to return to China. "I didn't like religion at first; I used to draw mustaches on the gods and mark the temples. But suddenly I was *gong* (the spirit entered my soul) and I became a priest." He won fame as a healer. Cures even of insanity and epilepsy were attributed to him. When he returned to Hawaii he had no intention of continuing this practice. "I tried to look for a job, but after securing one for a while, I would get sick and couldn't go back to work. . . . The gods wanted me to be a priest, so I had to become one or I would be unlucky and have many accidents."

The most conspicuous reminders to all Honolulu of the Chinese element in its blend of cultures are ceremonial observances, such as holidays and "rites of passage." No one in Honolulu—at least during the years before Pearl Harbor—could fail to overhear the two Chinese New Year's celebrations—one according to the haole calendar, the other according to a Chinese calendar officially obsolete in China, but still observed by the more conservative in Hawaii. The inescapable part of the celebration was the crackle of great strings of firecrackers. At other times the sound of firecrackers might denote almost any joyous occasion among the Chinese, particularly a wedding. Every spring at the Ching Ming

festival the Chinese cemeteries, where many of the older
generation lie on alien soil, swarm with their relatives and
descendants, who prepare a feast and a variety of other
offerings for them—candles, incense, and the inevitable
firecrackers. The occasion is well enough known to have
acquired a local name—Chinese Memorial Day or Chinese
Decoration Day. The harvest festival or moon festival,
which comes in mid-August by the haole calendar, is
similarly known as Chinese Thanksgiving. The public
at large receives notice of its coming through the appearance in Chinese store windows of round "moon cakes,"
filled with various kinds of Chinese mincemeat. The faithful hold a feast—enhancing the similarity to American
Thanksgiving—and toast the full moon.

Most spectacular of all are the funerals which honor
the passing of notable members of the immigrant generation. Incense and chanted prayers may last all night
and most of the day. When they are over, a huge funeral
procession winds through the streets, accompanied by
one or more Chinese bands playing the peculiarly strident
funeral music. This is said to be intended to scare away
evil spirits. If so, it is well adapted to its end. To make
doubly sure, zigzag strips of paper may surround the
hearse and be strewn along the way to baffle demons who,
it is believed, cannot turn a corner. At the cemetery, paper
replicas of everything the departed may need on his last
journey—money, servants, horses or, lately, automobiles
—are burned at the grave. Scrolls bearing tribute to his
virtues are set up on bamboo staffs about a pavilion which
covers the coffin. Offerings of food and—apparently an
adaptation from haole custom—a profusion of flowers,
surround the grave.

In the preservation of these ceremonies a number of values are involved. Familiarity is one of them, show another. Besides, each ceremony has one or more values of its own. It may express a sentiment for which haole culture affords no expression. Some of the ritual may be enjoyed for its beauty, some of it—like the firecrackers— just for fun.

These illustrations show that even those who voluntarily settled in Hawaii brought a great deal of China with them, and kept it alive. The details just cited emphasize conservatism rather than change. Yet there are suggestions of change even there. And other illustrations might be used to show how extensive the changes have been, particularly with some individuals. One extreme case will help to balance the picture. An old immigrant told M. Sing Au, in an interview for the *Mid-Pacific Magazine:* "I want to be buried in Manoa. I want to be there with my children and my children's children." Manoa is the site of the largest Chinese cemetery in Honolulu. This attachment to posterity rather than to the past amounts almost to a break with the ancestors and the land hallowed by their bones.

Japanese immigrants came to Hawaii under circumstances broadly similar to those of the Chinese, but with some differences that will need watching. As with the Chinese, those who returned home were clearly untouched by haole prestige. Among those who stayed, it is not possible in the case of the Japanese to make a distinction between voluntary and involuntary settlers, because there has not been among the Japanese anything corresponding to the Chinese Old Men's Home. There are several reasons for this. One is the more recent arrival of the Japanese; not so many of them have grown too old to work. Another is the larger proportion of women among them. Some immigrated with their husands, others came later as "picture brides." More women meant more children growing up in time to provide homes for the immigrant parents in their old age.

The greater proportion of women among the Japanese also meant the establishment of more Japanese households which, clustering in the same neighborhoods for the sake of company, developed little Japanese communities which had a fuller life than the Chinatowns, with their considerable bachelor population, could manage. In such enclaved communities gossip is an edged weapon, enforcing conformity to prevalent standards and retarding adoption of new ways.

On the other hand, the hard life of plantation workers was a strong inducement to adopt one American standard —that of getting on in the world. This was a radical change from the Japanese standard of carrying along a traditional occupation and role in society. This is, of course, a manifestation of the value of utility, perhaps combined with a touch of haole prestige. On this point W. C. Smith cites a Hawaiian-born young man: "My parents always told me to study hard and become a great man and not a cane-field laborer, who has to go to work early in the morning, rain or sun, and work to late in the evening."

An example of success in an enterprise of their own was set by the Japanese fishermen, who came to Hawaii independently of the plantation hands. Mankichi Murakami, on his way to the American mainland during the 1890's, happened to notice, while his ship was in Honolulu Harbor, the small and to his mind inefficient canoes used by the Hawaiians who were at that time supplying the city with fish. He wrote to his friend Goroki Naka-suki, enterprising descendant of a line of fishermen of Wakayama prefecture that here was a good opportunity for his trade. Nakasuki, who had been thinking of going to Australia, decided to try Hawaii instead. He invested his savings in a sampan, brought it to Hawaii in December, 1899, and took it out after bonito, the fish taken in greatest quantity in Hawaiian waters. His vessel, roomier than Hawaiian canoes, could hold more live bait, stay out longer, and bring in a bigger catch.

Once well started, Nakasuki so increased the supply of bonito in Honolulu that the price fell rapidly. He could still make money, but his Hawaiian competitors were hard hit. Some of them, the story goes, plotted to kill him at sea; but he was warned by Hawaiian friends and escaped. Later he branched out into fishing for *ahi*, called locally "Hawaiian tuna."

Word of this success brought many other Japanese fishermen to Hawaii. By 1901 they numbered about 200, and had 100 sampans; so the Japanese consul requested that a mooring place be set aside for them off the mouth of Nuuanu stream. A United States Government report for the same year said that they virtually monopolized deep-sea line fishing and were second to the Hawaiians in commercial fishing as a whole. Before long they took first place, and outstripped all competition, including some from haoles. They have been quick to take advantage of haole devices useful to them; putting in ice compartments instead of the live wells that made the early sampans logy sailors, and replacing sculls and sails with Diesel engines. But their contribution to choice among cultures as a whole was pretty surely to enhance Japanese rather than haole prestige.

During the immigration of "picture brides" (mainly 1907 to 1924) Japanese religion was changed in one respect by the compulsion of haole law. When the immigrants met their brides at the dock in Honolulu, though frequently they had never seen each other before, they regarded themselves as already married, because arrangements had been completed between their families in Japan. So they set up housekeeping without further ceremony. Among Americans, in whose culture the wedding ceremony is highly important as a sanctifier of sexual relations, there was an outcry about the supposed immorality of these apparently informal marriages. A regulation was adopted requiring that after the picture brides arrived a ceremony must be performed by a clergyman or magistrate. Any such rite was brand new to the Japanese, whose tradition wedding ceremony consists simply of bride and groom sipping nine times from the same cup of *sake*. The only witness is a young girl who brings the pot of sake into the room where the bride and groom sit, Japanese fashion. No priest has anything to do with it; in fact, the presence of a priest at a Japanese wedding is traditionally regarded as unlucky. But in response to the legal requirement, a ceremony was quickly improvised by Japanese priests for the immigrants and their "picture brides." At first it was performed at the wharf. Later the Izumo Taisha Temple, just off King Street in Honolulu, became headquarters for Japanese weddings. After the arrival of the last boatload of picture brides in 1924, more than 30 weddings were performed there in a single day.

Most of the importation of Japanese religion, however, naturally represented conservatism rather than change. The majority of the immigrants were followers of the Shinshu or Hongwanji sect of Buddhism. Subsidized in some instances by the plantations in the interest of contentment among the workers, temples of this and other sects were set up wherever Japanese settled in numbers. In this a number of values are involved: familiarity, the specifically religious solace, and probably compensation, to be discussed in detail later on. Although the state branch of Shinto, devoted to worship of the emperor and his divine ancestors, is not officially represented in Honolulu, the emotion-laden emphasis on Japanese ways and sentiments inseparable from worship in these temples undoubtedly tended to foster loyalty to Japan. Some details, particularly among the Shinto sects, linked religious and national sentiment more directly. The Daijingu shrine on Liliha Street was dedicated to nine deities regarded as ancestors of the imperial family; among them Amaterasu, the sun goddess. This shrine represented the branch of Shinto that centers in the ancient sanctuary at Ise, associated with the emperor's divine forebears. The Izumo Taisha Temple, which claimed in 1937 to be the only one retaining official connection with its Japanese headquarters (in this case the shrine at Izumo), had as one of its deities Susanoo, brother of Amaterasu. The Ishizuchi Jinsha, a less prominent shrine on King Street in the Moiliili district, was dedicated to a mountain god. His symbols are a jewel, a mirror, and a sword. Pamphlets issued by the temple in English explained that the jewel represents benevolence and healing; the mirror, enlightenment and prosperity; the sword, power and justice. But in Japan, jewel, mirror, and sword are the sacred imperial emblems, enshrined at Ise. It is hardly to be supposed that frequenters of the temple in Honolulu never remembered this.

Japanese surroundings, endeared by the value of familiarity, enhanced the appeal of the temples built for the immigrants. This is especially true of Shintoist temples, whose unpainted wood and archaic architecture are important not only esthetically but as religious symbols. Shintoist temples like the Daijingu shrine, set well back from Liliha Street, or the Izumo shrine, in the middle of a business block near the junction of King and Beretania Streets, were like transplanted bits of Japanese landscape. Some of the Buddhist temples preserved little of Japanese architecture; the comparatively new Hongwanji Temple on Fort Street, for instance, is more like a mosque than anything Japanese. Yet some of the more conservative Buddhist temples such as that of the Soto mission at School and Nuuanu Streets, made use of this appeal. Paul Tajima, in his study of Japanese Buddhism in Hawaii, noted a further development of the tendency in the temple of the Kenpon Hokke shu on upper Nuuanu Street, built during the 1930's: "The temple is arranged in Japanese style and the priest lives in Japanese fashion, which, perhaps, will give a more homelike feeling to the old Japanese." A pagoda-like tower surmounts the Makiki Christian church, where Reverend T. Okumura ministered to a congregation mainly Japanese.

Japanese teahouses expressed the same fondness for old-country surroundings. The construction of the first of them was recorded, and the feeling behind it expressed, by S. Sheba, editor of a Japanese newspaper, in a magazine article * written in 1911:

Two years ago T. Sakamoto, an aged amateur Japanese gardener, came to Honolulu. He had been an actor, was an artist. He longed for artistic Japan. His home was a Japanese club on School street by the Nuuanu stream. It was just an ordinary frame building surrounded by a common wooden fence, but Sakamoto performed a miracle. He lifted up a bit of old Japan and placed it down in Honolulu. He arranged an ideal garden, such as he had left behind, built a real Japanese tea house and erected an artistic Japanese fence with a torii gateway. Within this sacred corner, where Sakamoto spends his day, all is Japan.

Visitors come in their kimonos to tread on his polished floors and traverse the gravelled walks of his garden. At night friends come to dine on fish and vegetables that were brought all the way from Japan. Gay and gorgeous geisha girls serve and entertain the guests, as in Japan.

The Japanese of the territory saw, and admired. Other Japanese tea houses sprang up, built in real Japanese fashion, with gardens similar to those of the old country. In time it became necessary to send to Japan for a real professional landscape gardener from the famous district of Kumamoto, and now it is the thing among the Japanese of Hawaii to have real Japanese gardens in their grounds.

The occupations the Japanese took up when they left the cane-fields emphasize agriculture and crafts rather than business. In agriculture, they gradually took over from the aging Chinese a good share of the rice growing

* S. Sheba, "Japanese Home Life in Honolulu," *Mid-Pacific Magazine*, Vol. I, 1911.

and vegetable gardening. They achieved virtually a monopoly of coffee growing (chiefly in the Kona district of the island of Hawaii) and commercial flower gardening. A good many of the Okinawans specialized in raising hogs, a practice foreign to the culture of the rest of Japan. Among urban pursuits, the Japanese by 1928 had taken the lead in barbering, carpentry, clothes cleaning, dressmaking, and automobile repairing (the last a specialty of the Hawaiian-born generation).

Several reasons can be suggested for the comparative slowness of the Japanese to go into shopkeeping. One is that opportunities for little shops may have been largely preëmpted by the Chinese, as big business was by the haoles. Another is that shopkeeping takes more capital than most of the occupations listed above. A third may be a traditional Japanese ranking of occupations, by which military service (the profession of the *samurai*) stood highest, farming next, then arts and crafts, with commerce last and lowliest, except for occupations contaminated by association with death (butchering, tanning, gravedigging), which were relegated to the despised *eta*. The social standing of merchants in the Japan from which the immigrants came was, at best, like that of "tradesmen" in Victorian England rather than "businessmen" in the United States. An illustration of this contempt for trade came out during the negotiations for Japanese immigration to Hawaii. Japan refused to recognize the American-born Eugene Reed as minister plenipotentiary of the Hawaiian monarchy, giving as the reason, in a letter to him, the fact that "during your long residence in Japan you have been engaged in trade as a merchant here. . . . At any time when the Hawaiian government shall appoint a person not engaged in trade in this country to represent it, the government of Japan will make the treaty in the same manner as has been done with other foreign powers." As a matter of fact, the histories suggest that this may have been only an excuse to cover other objections to Reed. Nevertheless, Japan had that excuse ready to hand. Presumably the low rating of trade was one factor in Japanese preference for other occupations in Hawaii. But at length the high value attached to "business" in haole culture has joined with the value of utility, represented by profits, to make shopkeepers of the Japanese. During recent years their commercial undertakings have grown rapidly in numbers and importance.

The most conspicuous indication of persistence in the immigrant generation of a preference for Oriental culture was their establishment of Oriental language schools for their children. One of the principal motives for beginning the schools is said to have been an increasing difficulty in conversation between the immigrants and their Hawaiian-born children; another, an attempt to preserve such Oriental virtues as filial piety and family solidarity, which the immigrants found sadly lacking among the Hawaiian born. A third, in the case of schools established by Oriental religious sects, was of course the inculcation of Oriental religions. A fourth was undoubtedly, at least in some cases, loyalty to the ancestral nation and the wish to perpetuate that sentiment among the Hawaiian born.*

* The history of the issue that developed about these schools, the protests against them as an anti-American influence, and the resulting legislation, litigation, and concessions, have been reviewed with admirable impartiality by Ernest Wakukawa in *A History of the Japanese People in Hawaii*. The schools were suppressed after Pearl Harbor. It is doubtful whether any attempt will be made to revive them.

It is curious that the means chosen—establishment of schools—is more characteristic of haole than of Oriental culture. Still more curious that the first of the Japanese language schools, though established by a Japanese, Reverend Takie Okumura, was part of his work as a Christian missionary. The idea was quickly adopted by several Buddhist sects and other organizations. For our purpose, the Oriental language schools were significant mainly as evidence that haole prestige had not prevailed among a great many of the Oriental immigrants.

Choice between cultures is so intricate a process, or complex of processes, that to cover it with any approach to completeness, even in an individual case, would be a monumental task. In a study like this, that includes several large groups, there is no hope of marshaling the evidence exhaustively, or measuring one trend against another on any exact scale. What can be done, then, in the way of making out the direction and extent of cultural change among these immigrants? This much seems feasible: to strike a rough balance, indicating whether, after something like a half century in Hawaii, they were on the whole more American or more Oriental.

The conclusion submitted is that Oriental immigrants to Hawaii never swallowed haole prestige whole, as the Hawaiians of today have come near doing. While individuals among them range almost all the way from Oriental to American, the preponderance of choice appears to favor Oriental rather than American ways. This point has been made emphatically by John Embree in *Acculturation among the Japanese of Kona, Hawaii*:

For people of Kona, Japan, the native land, has a mystic power, a mana. Those who are born there possess a spirit, a character which is lacking among those born abroad. Furthermore, those born in Japan who have lately revisited the land of the gods have renewed and strengthened their mana. The word of such persons carries an added weight in the affairs of Kona. This sacredness extends to the language. A person who speaks the mother tongue well has much greater prestige than one who does not.

If the strength of this sentiment could be measured in various parts of Hawaii, there can be little doubt that it would be found to grow weaker along any line from such a segregated stronghold of Japanese influence as Kona toward the center of American influence, Honolulu. In the absence of such comparative measurement, the evidence at hand suggests that a good deal of the sentiment is left among Japanese immigrants throughout Hawaii, even in Honolulu itself. The rather scanty evidence assembled here about both Chinese and Japanese immigrants suggests a tentative generalization: that human beings transplanted to a new cultural environment when they are already mature tend to adopt the new culture only piecemeal, and to continue following in fundamentals (to just what extent will of course vary with many circumstances) the beliefs and behavior instilled in them in childhood rather than those that prevail in their new surroundings.

IV

The Growth of Haole Prestige among Children of Oriental Immigrants

CHILDREN of the immigrants who stayed in Hawaii were born into Oriental families—for we have just found that the parents remained more Oriental than American—but into an American community. Their youth was a tug of war between the two traditions. We already know which tradition won. The young Americans of Japanese parentage proved that in the war between the country of their ancestors and that of their own birth. If the similar war record of island-born Chinese in the American forces has been less noticed, that is mainly because the war did not raise the same issue with them, China and the United States being allies. Besides, they were not organized in separate units, so their performance did not stand out so distinctly from that of other Americans.

However, merely knowing which tradition won does not answer the question we are asking. That question is, how did the American tradition come to win? How did the shift from one traditional way of life to another come about, not through a century and a half of cumulative pressure, as with the Hawaiians, but during the few years of youth of the second generation? To answer that, we will have to examine more closely the tug of war as it went on during the early years of those now grown. It must be borne in mind all along that we are dealing with a wide range of individual behavior, and are trying to explain only the predominant choice. Some tendencies in the opposite direction, here viewed as no more than backwaters or eddies in the main stream, will be examined later.

It was the Oriental tradition that began to pull first. The Hawaiian born, both Chinese and Japanese, were brought into the world—commonly by midwives rather than physicians—in a flurry of old-country custom. Relatives sent gifts of clothing and the parents reciprocated with gifts of traditionally appropriate food. The baby was taken to a temple to be blessed. Baby clothes were of Oriental design, and among the Chinese, little bangles on the cap, and little jade bracelets, served not only for ornaments, but as amulets to ward off evil. The same atmosphere continued to surround the children throughout the early years that are considered so vital to the formation of character. Their world consisted mainly of their parents, and their parents brought them up mainly toward an Oriental way of life.

Glimpses of this influence are given in articles written by second-generation students in *Social Process in Hawaii*, published annually by the Sociology Club of the University of Hawaii. In "Some Forms of Chinese Etiquette in Hawaii" (1935) Alice Lee wrote: "Years ago, as a child, I can remember having to sweep the house early in the morning, heat water, and carry it in an elaborately designed wash basin to my mother's personal wash table. Her toothbrush, powder or paste, and towel must be laid conveniently at hand ready for use. Thus I was taught to reverence my parents."

In "The Second Generation Japanese and the Hong-wanji" Katsumi Onishi wrote:

The child in the average Buddhist family in Hawaii comes under the influence of the parental religion at an early age. He sees his parents go into the garden to pick the daily *o-hana* (flowers) for the *Butsudan* (Buddha's shrine). He watches his mother reverently offer fresh rice to the shrine and soon learns that no rice is to be eaten unless some of it is first offered on the altar. With the flowers and rice before the shrine and two small candles lighted on either side of the *butsudan*, the morning worship begins. He may join in the service, imitating his parents, as they offer the prayer of thanksgiving (*Namu Amida Butsu*), burn incense, and bow in deep reverence before the altar. He gazes interestedly at the flickering candles, delights in the melodious "ching-ching" of the tiny gong and plays aimlessly with the beads on the rosary. When father lets him light the candles and burn the incense, he is delighted. He asks his father to let him blow out the candles after the worship. . . . Long before the child enters either the public or the language school, he starts attending Sunday school with his elder brother or sister or a neighboring friend. The temple, beautifully decorated with flowers, candles and much gold lacquerwork, impresses him far more than his own family shrine. He listens to the organ, to the *gathas* (hymns) and learns to sing them in his own childish way. He listens to the tales of Buddha, of Shinran the founder of his sect, to exciting adventure stories, fables, and myths. He meets new faces, makes new friends, learns to revere and respect the Buddha. He anxiously looks forward to the *o-sagari-mono*, usually candy distributed to the pupils after it has been offered on the temple altar. Sunday is a day of joy, of fun, and of new and exciting experiences for him.

While there are hints of haole influence in both of these accounts, the predominance of Oriental influence is clear. It hardly seems necessary to illustrate in more detail how steadily these children were pulled toward Oriental culture during most of their waking hours.

But the moment they stepped into the world outside of their homes, or at any rate beyond their immediate neighborhoods, the Hawaiian born found themselves in the midst of modern America. Haole culture was not presented to them a little at a time, as it had been to the Hawaiians. It was presented as a functioning and dominating whole. So the choice they faced was not so much between particular practices, to be determined by specific values like utility and show. It was rather between two whole ways of life. Consequently even choices in detail often could not be decided separately, on their individual merits. Each appeared rather as an instance or manifestation of the underlying choice between two whole cultures. Many choices in detail were made unawares, as part of the process of drifting with the current. Even when particular choices were made consciously, they had to be governed at least as much by prestige as by whatever specific values might apply.

The pull of haole tradition reached full strength soon after the children entered school. This they were required by law to do at the age of six, as elsewhere in the United States. From then on they were subjected for six hours a day, five days a week, to what the Department of Public Instruction prescribed as preparation for American life. Even outside of school they were exposed, more and more as time went on, to agencies which were in effect engaged in disseminating haole ways: newspapers, motion pictures, radio—most of all the continuous performance of American life going on about them wherever they went. Outside of their homes haole prestige was rarely questioned.

Their new playmates, with most of whom haole prestige was a dogma, would attack anything conspicuously Oriental about them with ridicule—about as powerful a sanction as can be imposed on a child. The authority of these playmates was increased by several considerations. For one, being all about the same age and in about the same circumstances, they had a great deal in common which the parents did not share. For another, the new associates represented to some extent the wide world beyond home and neighborhood. This world, just now dawning on the children and apparently limitless in extent and power, exerted an influence that could no longer be rivaled by parents. The children had already repeatedly fathomed the limitations of the old folks, as children will do in spite of parental bluffs and stratagems. Moreover, these parents cut no imposing figure in the wide new world. If anything, they seemed lost and bewildered in it. So on the playgrounds of Hawaii, as on other American playgrounds, faith in parental infallibility did not last long. It was soon replaced by that American article of faith—that whatever is done by most of the people round about is the right and only thing to do. In Hawaii this meant acceptance of haole prestige.

The resulting break between immigrant and Hawaiian-born generations runs through almost every detail of behavior. It shows in their very names. Among the Chinese, the island born generally turn their names around in haole fashion, putting the family name last. And the "given" name is commonly a haole one. To take the first example from the "Who's Who" section of *The Chinese of Hawaii*, Samuel K. Young is the son of Young Yet Bo. Among the Japanese, even the immigrants commonly put the family name last; but the break between generations is evident in another way. Members of the second generation commonly have two "given" names: a Japanese one given by their parents, and a haole one chosen by themselves. At home, Masao; at bat, Jim. At home, Fumiko; in school, Violet. Among themselves the name most used is the haole one. Commonly both names go on their wedding certificates. When third-generation babies arrive, they may still get a Japanese name, if only to please their grandparents. But they also get a haole one to begin with.

Another conspicuous index of change, however trivial in itself, is the way the island born do their hair. It showed first among Chinese boys, in the days when their parents took for granted the wearing of a queue. This exposed Hawaiian-born boys not only to ridicule but to any number of painful pranks. A good many of them decided that parental wrath—however dreadful in Chinese tradition —was a lesser evil than continual humiliation, and the necessity of winning any respect they could get among their playmates by using their fists. So these bold spirits ventured to have their queues cut off. The parents could not do much more than fume about it. However, this particular issue between generations died out soon after 1912, when the revolution in China brought with it the abolition of the queue. The change soon spread to Hawaii, granting to the island born the boon of American haircuts.

Japanese males in Hawaii have, from the first, worn their hair cropped like haoles. The first shipload of immigrants, in 1868, did begin their journey with long hair, worn in the topknot familiar to Americans through old Japanese prints. But before they arrived, all but two of them had cut off their topknots as a thanks offering to the gods for escape from a storm at sea. And during the long interval before the second shipload arrived, in 1885, topknots were abolished in Japan by imperial decree.

So among the Japanese it has been only the girls who could show departure from ancestral custom by the way they wore their hair. A good many of them—more and more as time went on—have made the most of the opportunity. So for that matter have the island-born Chinese girls. A common sight in Honolulu, for at least a decade before Pearl Harbor, was a girl whose dress was Oriental, or partly so, and her features wholly so, but whose hair was bobbed and crimped in a "permanent wave," than which nothing could be more haole.

In a special Japanese Golden Jubilee edition of the Honolulu *Star-Bulletin* (1935), a page of pictures showing "Younger Japanese Who Are Prominent in Business Circles" included five young women—all proprietors of beauty shops. This curling of naturally straight hair illustrates haole prestige just as the opposite procedure—straightening of naturally tight-curled hair—does among American Negroes. The two converge toward the low wave of the whites.

With some Japanese individuals, Nature herself departs from the approved standard by giving the hair a natural wave. In old Japan this was a calamity, as readers of *A Daughter of the Samurai* may recall. But in twentieth-century Hawaii, when one third-generation girl was born with wavy hair, it was the Japanese grandmother herself who sighed "Well—it will save the expense of a beauty parlor."

After school, and on Saturday mornings, many of the immigrants' children attended Oriental language schools, which reinforced the pull of Oriental tradition. As to whether this could overcome the American pull, some evidence has already been presented. Attendance at Japanese language schools certainly failed to make their pupils (with rare exceptions) loyal to Japan rather than to the United States, if indeed the schools tried to do that. (The evidence suggests that they did, especially at first; but that as time went on they yielded more and more to American pressure.) The schools succeeded no better—or not much better—in their immediate task of preserving the ancestral language. A student in one of Professor F. M. Keesing's classes at the University of Hawaii suggests the outcome among island-born Chinese (1935): "The language used in the church has always been Chinese, but in the past three years English sermons are preached monthly because of the insistent demand of the younger generation. In most of the Chinese churches in Honolulu there has been a conflict between the old generation members and the younger members who claim they cannot understand the sermon preached in Chinese."

As for the Japanese, the University of Hawaii has been unable to find graduates of the language schools sufficiently versed in Japanese to be useful in cataloguing Japanese books for the university library. Only *kibei* (educated in Japan) qualified for this. One of Professor Keesing's students pointed out another indication (1935):

"The gradual decrease in the Oriental section of the Japanese newspapers, with accompanying increase in English pages, shows the decline of the Japanese language." Inability of the two generations to converse freely, for lack of a language mastered by both, has been a common difficulty, already mentioned from the parents' point of view. The children's point of view, in extreme form, is expressed in the pertly American comment of one youngster, quoted by Masuoka in his thesis on "Race Attitudes of the Japanese People in Hawaii": "We speak English among ourselves because it is a much easier language to speak than Japanese, but to our parents we must speak in Japanese. So we don't speak to them very often."

To be sure, the English which is the readiest means of communication among the Hawaiian born has a queer sound to mainland ears.* Its peculiarities are even, to some extent, kept up deliberately, and youngsters who abandon it for "standard American" may be condemned as affected, "haolefied." The attitude behind that will be discussed later. The point here is that the Hawaiian born do speak English rather than an Oriental language, from choice, among themselves. Moreover, when they want to, a good many of them can use English remarkably well. Quotations from their writings in these pages are proof enough of that. To give one more example, in 1935 Ah Sing Ching of Ewa, Oahu, 13 years old, won first prize in a nation-wide contest conducted by the American Legion

---

* Hawaiian English is analyzed by John Reinecke in "Language and Dialect in Hawaii": University of Hawaii, thesis for degree of Master of Arts, 1935. For briefer treatment, see Reinecke and Tokimasa, "The English Dialect of Hawaii," *American Speech*, Vol. 9, Nos. 1 and 2, 1934.

for essays on "How the Legion Can Best Serve the Nation."

When it comes to religion, the island-born Chinese have run true to form by abandoning the ways of their ancestors. The predominating tendency among them is brought out by Miss Sau Chun Wong in her study of "Chinese Temples in Honolulu" (*Social Process in Hawaii*, 1937): "The worshippers at the temples are chiefly first generation women. . . . Now, since the advent of Christianity, modern science, and public education, the older type of Chinese worship has ceased to control the life of a large part of the second and third generations of the Chinese community of Honolulu. The first generation go to the temples on feast days, a few consistently, while the younger generations seldom do." This conclusion is borne out by other witnesses.* Professor Shaochang Lee, who during his years at the University of Hawaii got to know the island born as well as anyone, declared (to trust to memory of a statement made orally): "The younger Chinese are either Christians or agnostics."

An extreme case of the break between generations in this respect, and one clearly motivated by haole prestige, comes out in a statement by an island-born girl, quoted by W. C. Smith in *Americans in Process:*

Unfortunately, to say the least, my mother is still unconverted . . . I have always condemned her worship and offerings, and sometimes I have made fun of my smaller brothers and sisters. She forces them to bow before the incense and my fifteen year old brother has stopped because, when he

---

* Hsieh T'ing-yu, "The Chinese in Hawaii," *Chinese Social and Political Science Review*, 1930. Fred K. Lam, "A Survey of the Chinese in Hawaii," *Mid-Pacific Magazine*, 1929.

was about thirteen years old, I called him a "heathen Chinese" after he had bowed. . . . We live in a district that has no other Chinese family and sometimes when it's full moon or some other festival day, mother pops firecrackers and burns incense. Some of my neighbors have teased me and I do not find it pleasant to have my friends see the little shrine that she has built in the kitchen.

The choice of religion among Hawaiian-born Japanese is strikingly different. During the 1930's Shinshu or Hongwanji Buddhism was numerically the strongest religious sect in Hawaii. In an article already quoted, Katsumi Onishi said (1937): "Of the 28,000 adherents, more than half are second generation Japanese with American citizenship." Here is certainly an upstream choice. One obvious reason for it is the fact that the Hongwanji, unlike the go-as-you-please Chinese temples, is a highly organized institution with a strong missionary bent, and carries on a continuous campaign to keep the Hawaiian born within the fold. Another and more significant reason, which will be discussed in the next chapter, is that the ancestral religion is strong in the value of relief from haole dominance. Still other values, that of familiarity, for one, are involved. The question here is, what does this show about acceptance of haole prestige?

It shows, certainly, that haole prestige had not been completely and universally accepted, reminding us once more that we are dealing with a wide range of behavior. As to that, choice in religion included Christianity and various degrees of indifference, as well as Buddhism in several forms. No satisfactory count of heads could be obtained. But the numbers of Christians, in Honolulu alone, included the second-generation membership of five Japanese Christian congregations, besides members of Japanese descent in other Christian churches. In particular, nisei made up a large part of the membership of the Church of the Crossroads, near the University of Hawaii. As for agnostics, atheists, or the apparently larger number whose attitude is the common American one of indifference to all religion, there are no grounds for even an estimate of their numbers. But at least they were not hard to find. One Hawaiian-born young man said, in answer to a question about his own preference in religion, "I don't pay any attention to those things." Casual observation suggests that this was a very common attitude.

One point that seems clear, even without a count of heads, is that while Buddhism had more adherents than Christianity among the Hawaiian born, Christianity had more than Shinto. On this, one of Professor Keesing's students said (1935): "The tending of votive shelves, pilgrimages to ancestral graves and the keeping of anniversaries of the deaths of kinsmen are practices that mean little or nothing to local young Japanese. Japan's own religion, Shintoism . . . has practically no hold on their lives. As far as these young people are concerned, the family religious cult is dead." A Hawaiian-born young woman said that, insofar as household worship did continue, it meant to her, and she thought to most of her generation, an expression of family solidarity rather than of any feeling that she would call religious.

On certain holidays, especially New Year's, considerable numbers of Hawaiian-born Japanese used to attend Shinto temples. When one of the friends who helped with this study expressed the common opinion that the

Hawaiian born took little interest in Shinto, I asked him about these holiday gatherings. Himself California born of Japanese parentage, he was then living in one of the most Japanese neighborhoods in Honolulu, and I believe his reply expressed an attitude quite general among nisei. He said:

These young people go to the temples just because other people go. They want to be with the crowd. They have nothing religious in their minds. They don't pray; oh, a few words maybe, but nothing serious. You know, these young people are getting smart! They want facts, not enchantments. But when you get old, you have nothing to rely on. Then you rely on these things.

Take me, I do not belong to any religion. But now that my wife is in the hospital, some of the neighbors have offered to take me to a temple. So I go. I ask the priest to make prayers for her. I don't know if it does any good or not. It is like mental healing.

Finally, the methods adopted by the Hongwanji sect, stronghold of Japanese religion in Hawaii, to appeal to the Hawaiian born include wholesale borrowings from Christian apparatus and procedure. There is a Sunday school, complete with blackboard, illustrated lesson books, charts, and hymns. There is a Y.B.A., as much like the Y.M.C.A. and Y.W.C.A. as the initials suggest. There is a wedding service performed by a priest, an innovation in which the Buddhists followed, after a long interval, the lead of the Shinto priests who improvised a wedding ceremony in the days of "picture brides." The ritual follows Christian precedent closely, even to closing with the following benediction: "May wisdom and compassion arise within your hearts. Peace be unto you."

Paul Tajima, in his study of "Buddhism in Hawaii," comments: "In what sutra do we find such an expression?"

Americanized Buddhism in its extreme form, and the impression it made on an observer accustomed to a more conservative kind, were vividly described by Souno Inouye, who used to be known as "the sage of Kona" in the days when he wrote correspondence from that remote district for the Honolulu *Advertiser*. In 1928 he left his coffee plantation, revisited Honolulu, took in the sights, and published his impressions in the paper. This is what he had to say about "a haole Buddhist service at the largest Hongwanji temple in the islands":

Entering the minareted edifice we were rather bewildered to hear an ample-tone organ melody, nicely played by a blonde young lady clad in a light-green satin dress, crowned with a stunning white hat. Both the organist and her sonorous instrument potently hinted a Christian service, and we rubbed our narrow eyes, wondering if it could be a Buddhist function. Any one born and bred in a Buddhist circle in Asia always associates brocade-robed brown priests, huge bronze gongs, kneeling worshippers, and solemn chanting of "namu-ami-dabu" with all rites and ceremonies honoring the serene divinity upon the lotus throne. Likewise in vain our wandering gaze sought for the traditional gilded and carved images of dragons, symbolic lotuses, angelic beings gliding through clouds, and other soothing forms embellishing the ancient temples of Asia. But these immemorial trappings were noticeable by their utter absence, though the Fort street edifice is fairly large. So this admirer of old-fashioned Buddhism was rather disenchanted.

Following the organ prelude came hymn-singing in English, led by another haole lady equally attractive. By the way, those anthems in the Americanized "hymnal" closely resemble typical Protestant hymns—in sentiments, cadence, phrasing, and stanza structure. Frequently occurring in the "Englished" book of praise are such familiar phrases as "Love Divine," "Gracious Master," "Holy Law," and "Perfect Bliss," etc. (These oft-repeated phrases are always printed in capitals.) The similarities are explained easily by the fact that the hymns sung at the temple were composed mostly by talented Anglo-Saxon followers of the Oriental faith, mostly of the gentler sex. In strict poetic merit, however, these Buddhist hymns are perhaps no worse than the average Protestant anthem of praise.

Indeed, if the vital words "Dharma" and "Buddha" were replaced by "Savior" and "Jesus," those Buddhist songs might be acceptable in any orthodox Protestant hymnal. That's how near Americanized Buddhism approaches Christianity.

After the opening hymn a Nordic gentleman led in a responsive reading—another adoption of Christian service, unknown to pure-bred Buddhism. Then following a demure choiring by young Japanese girls in their adopted language, came an address by a fluent blonde lady, with a pleasing intonation. She was effectively attired in a white, sleeveless dress and a black necklace.

The theme of her oration was that arch-American, Henry Ford. She sought to prove that the flivver magnate's philosophy of life, his well-advertised agnostic creed, was essentially the same as that of her Lord Buddha. We fancy that novel interpretation of his faith would highly entertain the affluent Henry.

Excepting for the presence of a glittering shrine and the abstinence from any "offertory" caroling (for which our slender purse offered mighty thanks), this Buddhist ceremony glided along much like the usual church service. And the congregation resembled the one we joined at the Church of the Crossroads a week previous—composed in the main of Oriental young folks with a sprinkling of *haole* elders. Putting a finishing Occidental touch, the winsome organist ushered out the worshipping throng with a postlude of Teutonic melody.

Katsumi Onishi found that even this Americanized Buddhism, though numerically stronger than any other church in Hawaii, fails to hold many of the Hawaiian born as they mature.

When the boy approaches junior high school age, Sunday school often loses its charm, and as he gets older, he drifts away more and more. The stories are not interesting enough, or other attractions, usually athletics, demand his time and attention. He may also consider family worship as something childish and neglect to join in the services. Approximately two-thirds of the boys lose touch with the temple when they drop out of Sunday school at adolescence. On the other hand, the Sunday school has a firmer hold on the average adolescent girl. . . . Later with increasing duties at home, the girls likewise tend to drop out of Sunday school.

We are now in a position to answer with some confidence the question: "What does the continuing strength of Buddhism show about acceptance of haole prestige?" Clearly it does not show, as might have been supposed at first glance, an outward conformity to haole ways, cloaking a Japanese spirit within. Insofar as it is not itself merely a matter of outward form, of being carried along by the momentum of an established routine, it is simply one of the ways in which the Hawaiian born of Japanese descent can cherish something of their ancestral culture, while remaining predominantly American.

In play time the Hawaiian born went in for American sports. The contrast between generations in this respect was perhaps sharper among the Chinese, for the Chinese immigrants were rather averse to athletics. Although Chinese boxing, which seems to run to calisthenics more than to combat, had some devotees among them, their favorite recreation was gambling. Among their sons, gambling did not lose all its appeal; but athletics, in American forms, has been decidedly more in evidence. Loui Leong Hop, sports writer for the Honolulu *Star-Bulletin*, wrote a "History of Chinese Sports in Hawaii" for the 1929 edition of *The Chinese of Hawaii*. By "Chinese sports" he meant American sports played by descendants of Chinese. The various Chinese baseball clubs, which have sent teams on tour to the American mainland and the Orient, got most attention. On the sporting pages of Honolulu newspapers, Chinese names have been especially prominent in tennis. Their showing has been well up to average in most other sports as well, from golf through basketball to boxing. In football, average light weight puts the Chinese at a disadvantage against haoles and Hawaiians. Yet they hold their own in the celebrated "barefoot leagues" of Hawaii, where teams are classified according to weight. Not infrequently a football player of Chinese stock makes the first team at the University of Hawaii. Only in water sports is there any perceptible remnant of the ancestral lack of interest in athletics.

In the case of the Japanese, the immigrants were anything but averse to athletics. They organized clubs for the practice of *sumo* wrestling, jiujitsu, fencing with bamboo foils, and archery. The Hawaiian-born generation retained some interest in these, especially in *judo*. (Judo itself, being a sportsmanlike variant of the earlier and deadlier jiujitsu, reflects European influence in Japan.)

But there is no question that American sports have been far more popular. On that, a witness whom nobody would suspect of pro-American bias is the Buddhist priest Tetsuo Tachibana. As head of the physical training department of the Hongwanji High School, most advanced of Japanese language schools, he was before the war the foremost proponent of Japanese sports. His specialty was judo, in which he held high rank. Yet he ruefully admitted to William Maxwell (Honolulu *Star-Bulletin*, December 19, 1936): "*Judo* lacks popularity because it is an indoor sport, giving pleasure mostly to the participants. The niceties of the game, the mental control, the spirit of give and take, can be appreciated only by the players themselves. American sports, on the other hand, are more carefree. They are material pleasures, giving enjoyment to the spectators as well as the players."

As this comment suggests, the choice of American sports among the sons of Japanese involved more than just a preference for one form of exercise or amusement over another. Nor was it merely another manifestation of haole prestige, though that may well have been the deciding value. The factor of special interest in this choice is a difference in spirit between the athletic sports of the two cultures. For one thing, the contestants in Japanese sports are individuals rather than teams. Where the Americans emphasize teamwork, the Japanese emphasize individual discipline. Moreover, in Japanese athletics, as one young devotee of their archery said, "The spiritual side is the most important." In this solemn atmosphere the unrestrained American delight in winning the game, in the presence of a roaring crowd, would be quite out of place. Finally, with the exception of sumo, the Japanese sports originated as forms of military training. Behind their emphasis on self-control was the thought of its possible culmination in self-sacrifice on the field of battle. Your American youth, while as capable of sacrifice as any other if need be, plays games for fun, first of all; secondly, for exercise. If self-discipline comes in at all, it comes in a poor third. It is not a conscious goal. All this is as true of those whose parents were Japanese as of any others.

Thus throughout their school years the Hawaiian born of Oriental stock have become more and more American. The process was favored by an atmosphere kindlier toward their race, and more tolerant of racial and cultural differences, than that of the American mainland. But when they got out of school, and set out to win their way toward prosperity, as good Americans are expected to do, they met with a rude shock. They found that the tolerance and friendliness among races, for which Hawaii has been justly celebrated, prevailed only within limits, and at a price. The price demanded by the dominant haoles—never in so many words but nonetheless insistently—has been cheerful acceptance by other peoples of a subordinate place. Most haole residents have some claim—whether through their own qualifications, the influence of friends and relatives, or both—to employment in one of the more remunerative, or at least pleasanter kinds of occupation. Indeed, those who have no such claim—laborers and artisans—have been discouraged from settling in Hawaii by the fact that it was not, for them, "a white man's country." But to those safely installed in comfortable and remunerative jobs, it was a white man's country indeed; one of the best. They were more than willing to leave less desirable work to people of browner hue. In other words, racial friendliness in Hawaii has been helped by the fact that for a generation or two before Pearl Harbor, economic competition between races was negligible. The haoles were so sure of the best of everything that they could even see, without alarm, a few individuals of other stock rise well toward the top in business or the professions. But, unless the individuals were helped along by haoles (as was done for political reasons in some cases, from pure kindliness in others), they had to win their success against odds.

Most of the Hawaiian born have made the best of this situation. They have gone about making a living in whatever ways were open to them. The fact that these were mostly haole ways is not, of itself, evidence of haole prestige so much as of the fact that haole economic dominance left hardly any other ways open. Nor did the increasing prosperity of the Hawaiian born, and the shift in occupations from manual labor toward business and the professions, constitute another instance of the break between generations; for the immigrants themselves were not slow to take advantage of whatever economic opportunities they saw.

Still, even in this matter of occupations, the change between immigrants and Hawaiian born did show at some points. One was the increasing proportion of women among the breadwinners. Schoolteaching and stenography have been favorite occupations with Hawaiian-born girls. Among the Japanese, another change has been the disappearance of the old rating of occupations, by which the profession of arms was the most honorable, farming next, arts and crafts third, and trade or business at the bottom. One of Professor Keesing's students wrote: "The above classification has certainly lost its significance among the Japanese here in Hawaii. To the second generation it seems remote and strange. Stranger still is it to a Japanese father who on mentioning proudly the fact that he is of a *hyakusho* (farmer) family, notices his son take the remark with a shrug and a questioning uplift of the eyebrow."

The conflict between immigrant and Hawaiian-born generations—which is to say, between Oriental and American traditions—reached its climax on the question of whom to marry. To the Hawaiian born, steeped in the American ideal of romantic love, the most repugnant of all rules of Oriental tradition is that which confers on their families the prerogative of choosing mates for them.

It is hard to measure the course of change in this respect. To be sure, change is perceptible in all details of procedure. For example, Miss Anne Kuraoka, in an article called "No Less American," testified: "Where a kiss is considered ill-bred in Japan, Hawaiian-born sons and daughters enjoy all the sweet liberties that go with the pursuit of happiness." Miss Amy Akinaka, in *Social Process in Hawaii* (1935) reported in detail two wooings and weddings as examples of different stages in Americanization. William Maxwell, in an article based on painstaking inquiry ("Japanese-Americans Turn from Customs of Their Forefathers," Honolulu *Star-Bulletin* December 19, 1936), showed how the Hawaiian born were resisting the demands of their parents on a number of points, particularly the expense of meeting such a traditional requirement as a lavish feast after the wedding. This and other inquiries show that employment of a go-between in arranging a marriage was during the 1930's an obviously waning though by no means extinct custom.

Inquiry at the office of the Governor of Hawaii, during the course of this study, showed that one Japanese form of marriage was still not unusual. This is the so-called *yoshi* marriage. When only daughters were born to a family, it was considered necessary, in order to carry on the line and name, for the husband of the eldest daughter to join her family and take her name, instead of the other way about, which is the usual custom in Japanese as it is in haole culture. From 1931 to 1936 the governor issued 96 decrees of change of name to persons of Japanese descent. The petitions in a little more than a third of these cases (35) gave the *yoshi* custom as the reason. Thus: "Your petitioner states that according to an ancient custom of the Japanese people, it is customary to have the surname of the groom changed to that of the bride when marriage is solemnized under such circumstances as those under which your petitioner's was performed"; or "That the said —— desires to change his name to [bride's name] in order to carry on the name and pedigree of the family [bride's name], inasmuch as there are no male survivors to carry on the said name." Yet change in this respect, while not a matter of record, did take place in one family of my acquaintance. The husband of the oldest daughter joined her household, giving them the practical advantages of having a man about the place; but she took his name. Her father's family name is being allowed to die out. This decision may have been influenced by the fact that he was no longer living.

All this shows little more than that conflict and change

were going on, something we knew to begin with. It does not help much toward answering the crucial question: Who has been doing the choosing, the young people themselves or their families? In testifying where he stood on this issue, one of Professor Keesing's students (1935) probably spoke for a large percentage of his generation: "I, myself, am influenced by the Americanization program, and I don't intend to have my relationships controlled by my folks. However, this does not mean that I will not respect my dad, for the desire of respect has been bred within me and I will respect my dad always. What I mean is that my dad is not going to tell me how to live and how to carry on my personal relationships."

The issue was drawn most sharply, and with least chance for a compromise satisfactory to both generations, when two young people whose marriage would be forbidden by Oriental tradition nevertheless wanted to marry, because they had fallen in love in the American way. Chinese and Japanese families, in arranging marriages, were guided by a considerable body of rules. In China, for example, the exogamic principle, or incest prohibition, which appears in all cultures, took the extreme form of prohibiting marriage between persons of the same surname. The file of marriage licenses in Hawaii shows a few violations of this rule. I heard of one case, too, where a compromise was worked out. The letter of the law was observed by changing the spelling (in English letters) of one of the names. Another Chinese rule follows the opposite or endogamic principle—the principle that one should marry a person of one's own kind. One specific expression of this, in the Canton delta, was disapproval of marriage between Punti (old Cantonese) and Hakka. Violations of this rule, too, are not hard to find in Hawaii. Cases like these certainly indicate a weakening of Oriental tradition.

A wide range of behavior, from Oriental to American, can also be shown in observance of certain Japanese rules of an endogamic character. Of these, the most stringent is prohibition of marriage by other Japanese to a descendant of the *eta*—the caste whose members were, in old Japan, required to live in separate villages, and restricted to the most despised occupations. Feeling in Hawaii toward this group was discussed by one of Professor Keesing's students (1935).

The *eta*, or *Chorinbos*, are often called "four fingers" by the Japanese. . . . The Japanese people in Hawaii do not make the distinction overtly but they either condemn these people in soft whispers or hold up four fingers of one hand to indicate that so and so is of this caste. The minute four fingers are raised in any conversation, the parties thus informed give an understanding nod. . . . It seems that the caste system is dying out because the second generation Japanese do not see any difference between the people of this caste and the ordinary Japanese . . . However, there are some who still emphasize the stigma attached to a "Chorinbo."

In April, 1938, a Hawaiian-born boy and girl of Japanese descent committed suicide by throwing themselves overboard from a steamer on the way from Kauai to Honolulu. This is *shinju*, double suicide for love, a traditional Japanese way out for lovers whose families prevent their marriage. The girl's name indicated that she was of eta descent, though apparently she herself did not know it until the question of this marriage came up.

In evaluating this extreme case of victory of Oriental tradition it should be noted, first, that this kind of suicide is very rare in Hawaii. Shigehiro Kawamura, librarian of the newspaper *Nippu Jiji*, kindly looked up for me the cases in his files. He found only three others: the first at Hana on the island of Maui in 1908; the second at Koko Head, near Honolulu, in 1913; and the third at Waianae, Oahu, in 1919. The list may not be complete. But these suicides are so dramatic that they would be reported, as a rule, in the newspapers.

Community approval of this kind of suicide is indicated by the fact that a monument stands near the railway station at Waianae in honor of the two who drowned themselves there in 1919. But I was told by one of the oldest of the Hawaiian-born Japanese that a change in sentiment has been plainly perceptible since then. The 1938 case, he said, was generally regarded as a disgrace.

Letters left behind by this hapless pair show that the pull of American tradition was too strong, upon the girl at least, to leave her the consolation of regarding her desperate course as honorable. She wrote: "I believed those Medieval Ages could never be brought back to life in this year of 1938 but the surprising thing is they are much alive. . . . Ever since I learned about our heritage and its class, it completely altered the pattern of life I was leading. . . . The shocking news was too much for me—all those weeks of mental strain finally made me choose the road of cowardice, the lowest thing a person can do but to me it's the only happiness I know of." The boy wrote: "I'm doing this for my family. I love ——, but I'm going to sacrifice myself for all of you. I can't marry her." Apparently his attitude was the more Japanese of the two. Yet he repeatedly expressed the hope of being with her in heaven.

Two other factors should be considered in evaluating this case. In the first place, these young people came from rural Kauai, one of the remote regions where Oriental tradition has been least opposed by American influence. In the second place, the suggestion of suicide was undoubtedly made to them by the act of an American woman, depressed by long illness, who leaped overboard from the same boat only a few days before they did.

A case of the opposite extreme is furnished by at least one married couple in Honolulu. The husband is said to be of eta descent, the wife of higher caste. Whatever whispering the conservative may indulge in, his ancestry has not prevented him from becoming one of the most prosperous businessmen of Japanese descent in Honolulu.

Another striking instance of extreme American choices came out during a study which was a by-product of this one.* The marriages involved were between Hawaiian-born youth of Chinese and of Japanese descent. The strength of parental objection can be judged by the existence of a whole cluster of Japanese rules against marriage to persons of different local origin. The feeling seems to be that if the two families have been neighbors for generations, they know what kind of people they are dealing with, and what to expect at every turn in the new relationship. Hence it is considered preferable to marry into a family that came from the same village in Japan; failing that, at least from the same prefecture. The

* Edwin G. Burrows, *Chinese and Japanese in Hawaii during the Sino-Japanese Conflict* (Institute of Pacific Relations, Honolulu, 1939).

question of marriage to people from another island in Japan, let alone outside of Japan altogether, probably never came up in the old country. In Hawaii, where people from various parts of Japan, and of the world, have been thrown together, it comes up continually. Persistence of old standards shows especially in strong objection to marriage between a family from "Japan proper" and one from Okinawa.

From such a point of view, marriage to a Chinese would be literally outlandish. And the Chinese, in such matters, are fully as complacent as the Japanese (or the Americans). Moreover, in these particular cases, antagonism was warmed over, to put it mildly, by the fact that China and Japan were at war. Yet I was told by Riley H. Allen, editor of the Honolulu *Star-Bulletin,* that during the first year of open warfare in China, two young Chinese-Japanese couples had asked the newspaper not to publish issuance of their marriage licenses until after the weddings. The object was not to let the parents know until it was too late. Once married, the Hawaiian-born couples were willing to face the storm.

The extent and rate of change in this matter have been analyzed statistically by Romanzo Adams in *Interracial Marriage in Hawaii.* Of the Chinese he says, "In the not distant future it will be the custom for young people to make their own marriage arrangements. Some do this now and in other cases a son may really make his own choice while the parents go through the usual formalities of betrothal."

Of the Japanese: "The parents, despite their mistrust of American ways, recognize that their children are to be Americans and that they must adjust themselves to the practical situation. In a good many cases they begin by enforcing Japanese custom and end by yielding to their children. For example, in a certain family, the parents selected the husband of the eldest daughter; the second daughter rebelled, and the third was free to accept the man she might like. . . . The outlook is that the parental influence in the choice of brides and grooms will not survive the passing of the immigrant generation."

To summarize what seems to be the prevalent degree of acceptance of haole prestige among Hawaiian-born children of Orientals, I cannot do better than quote the wistful inquiry of a nisei girl who used to take care of our housekeeping in Honolulu before she had a household of her own. One day she said that she and her friends had been discussing the behavior of some rowdy youngsters of European stock who had got into trouble with the police. "The boys said these are not real haoles. What are real haoles?" Whatever distinction they may have had in mind (some distinguish between haoles and Portuguese), she and her friends were evidently groping for a definition of haole that would exclude those of whom they could not approve, and leave their faith in haole superiority intact.

Many of the Hawaiian born are far beyond such naïveté. But they, in their sophistication, are all the more American.

V

Haole Prestige among Haoles

IN the early days some haoles went native. Archibald Menzies, naturalist with Vancouver's expedition, visited the island of Kauai in 1792, and met there the sailor James Coleman, who had been left the year before to collect sandalwood for his ship. "This man made his appearance dressed like the natives, with only a malo round his waist, and indeed his skin was so sunburnt that he differed very little from them in color. He was tattooed with a broad badge over his left shoulder meeting low down on his left side." He seems to have liked this way of life, for later ships found him at Waikiki, entrusted by the chief there with the task of smoothing out relationships between Hawaiians and visiting haoles.

Kamehameha's celebrated advisers, Isaac Davis and John Young, though kept in Hawaii at first against their will, stayed on voluntarily, took native wives, and adopted to a great extent a native way of living. Desertions from haole ships became so frequent that for a time they were a problem both to shipmasters and to native chiefs. In 1825 Aaron Mitchell and others wrote from Nantucket to President John Quincy Adams, complaining that in Hawaii there were "over one hundred and fifty seamen . . . prowling about the country, naked and destitute, associating themselves with the natives, assuming their habits and acquiring their vices." Some of these men were discharged willingly by skippers who preferred Hawaiian foremast hands. Others, like Archibald Campbell, were disabled, and left in the islands to convalesce. A great many, apparently, were drunkards and vagabonds who, far from making a choice between Polynesian and haole cultures, were probably incapable of settling down to anything. Yet a few, like Young and Davis, seem to have been fairly capable men whose haole upbringing did not prevent them from deliberately adopting another way of life.

As to the values behind such a choice, there is very little on record. Vancouver wrote of Young and Davis: "The principal object they seemed to have in view was to correct by gentle means the vices and encourage by the same laudable endeavor the virtues of these islands." Peter Puget attributed to Young himself a more convincing explanation: "habituated to a Life of Ease and Tranquility, he did not like to launch once more into the Busy World where he was certain that the only Sustenance he could expect must be by hard Labour." This, the nearest to a first-hand account of the matter found, pretty surely points to one of the principal values—utility, in the form of creature comforts. A mariner's life was pretty hard in those days. The life of a guest among the Hawaiians was, by comparison, luxurious.

"Those who took up their abode with Hawaiians," wrote the missionary Hiram Bingham, "easily accustomed themselves to the native customs, morals, and mode of living." The point about morals doubtless names another value—ready sexual satisfaction, in contrast to the enforced celibacy of life aboard ship. Still another, in the case of men like Coleman, Davis, and Young, may well have been increased status and power. Though affairs of state in Hawaii were on a small scale, compared to those of European courts, the role of a haole mariner might be far more satisfying in the little island kingdom.

Values of a different kind may have influenced another haole who came to Hawaii on the same ship as James Coleman. This was "Padre" John Howell, the ex-clergyman who tried to convert Kamehameha. He had been clerk on the *Lady Washington;* but according to Menzies "came . . . with intent to remain some time in these Islands." Before that, he had been a wanderer, had lived for a time at Nootka on the American northwest coast, and visited China. Vancouver sums up his impression of Howell in this sentence: "He appeared to possess a good understanding with the advantage of a university education, and had once been a clergyman of the Church of England, but had now secluded himself from European society."

Why he should have chosen to do that is not on record, but there are some hints. Presumably a man of his standing at home did not come for creature comforts or higher status. Nor did he come as a missionary, although, if the story of his attempt to convert Kamehameha is true, he was not disillusioned with Christianity. However, a man of "sensibility" in those days may well have been disillusioned with haole civilization for other reasons. Reasons were in the air toward the end of the eighteenth century. Some of them had been eloquently expressed in books like those of Rousseau; and Howell was apparently a reader of books. He may have been brought to Hawaii by that complex and elusive lure, romance.

Even if the diagnosis does not fit this case, certainly romance has brought others to Hawaii, ever since

Howell's day. Perhaps the most articulate of romantic visitors was Robert Louis Stevenson. He had seen the Marquesas and Tahiti before he reached Hawaii, where he lived for only a few months, in 1889. Fragments from his letters show that if he liked the Hawaiian Islands less than some others, it was because Hawaii was by that time less Polynesian. "The Sandwich Islands do not interest us very much; we live here, oppressed with civilization, and look for good things in the future." Yet the letters show, too, that once away from Honolulu, he found in the remoter parts of Hawaii something of what he was looking for. Stevenson was able to say what it was he was looking for, as few can. For instance:

I have just been a week away alone on the lee coast of Hawaii, the only white creature in many miles . . . ; a lovely week among God's best—at least, God's sweetest works— Polynesians. It has bettered me greatly. If I could only stay there the time that remains, I could get my work done and be happy; but the care of my family keeps me in vile Honolulu, where I am always out of sorts, amidst heat and cold and cesspools and beastly haoles. What is a haole? You are one; and so, I am sorry to say, am I. After so long a dose of whites, it was a blessing to get among Polynesians again even for a week.

Stevenson could also say what he found wrong with haoles and their ways. He did so in a letter to W. H. Low:

But O Low, I love the Polynesian: this civilization of ours is a dingy, ungentlemanly business; it drops out too much of man, and too much of that the very beauty of the poor beast: who has his beauties in spite of Zola and Co. . . . But if you could live, the only white folk, in a Polynesian village; and drink that warm, light *vin du pays* of human affection, and enjoy that simple dignity of all about you . . . I will not gush, for I am now in my fortieth year, which seems highly unjust, but there it is, Mr. Low, and the Lord enlighten your affectionate

R. L. S.

Stevenson gladly went on to Samoa, where he could enjoy Polynesia in higher concentration. Though he would have gone back to Scotland before long, if he could, he still represents, in fully developed form, the kind of preference for a good deal in Polynesian life over haole life that can be called romantic.

What is romance, in this sense? What is the value, or cluster of values, that sends people, some kinds of people, to the South Seas? One value in it is novelty, for romance seems to attach especially to whatever is far away and different. Another is beauty; for whatever is thought of as romantic is thought of as beautiful in some sense; and the power of romance over individuals seems to vary with the importance of beauty to them. Witness the high proportion of artists and writers among romantic visitors to the South Seas—Melville, Loti, Gauguin, to mention only some of the best known. Witness also Stevenson's complaint against haole civilization, that it detroys "the very beauty" of man. This complaint suggests, too, a third value in romance—relief from any of a wide variety of dissatisfactions with life at home. With persons for whom novelty and beauty have a strong appeal, almost any dissatisfaction, if only it is strong enough, can kindle the romantic kind of longing. A Polynesian island is, of course, only one of the possible goals of this longing. To use the term most fashionable just now, romance in this sense is one way of escape, and escape is perhaps the strongest value in it.

Probably Hawaii has always had a few romantics in its haole population. A considerable number have felt the appeal of romance, as embodied in the vision of a South Sea island, enough to dream about it, talk about it, dabble with it; at very least, respond to a tourist advertisement and stay for a while at a tourist hotel. With a few, like Stevenson, this sentiment involved renunciation, at least partial and temporary, of haole prestige. From that extreme the importance of romance grades all the way down to that of a light diversion for leisure time.

Renunciation of haole culture in only one respect, but an important one, is represented by another still smaller group: haole converts to Buddhism. Around 1930 the bishop of the Hongwanji mission was a haole, M. T. Kirby; later there was another clergyman of English descent, Ernest H. Hunt, in the same Buddhist mission. The total number of haoles in the congregation was said to be about 100.

What values motivated that choice of Oriental over haole religion could only be determined by rather searching histories of each individual. Still, tentative suggestions can be made. Few nowadays would expect to find the deciding value in a reasoned preference for Buddhist over Christian doctrines. Even if the matter appeared to the convert himself in that light, others would suspect behind the decision, even behind the comparison, some emotional impulse; some dissatisfaction with haole culture or with the individual's experience of it. In other words, these converts to Buddhism, though admittedly seen only from the outside, seem to resemble the romantics in a tendency to escape, not only into religion, which is everywhere man's last resort, but into a form of religion remote from that of their early life, which had somehow failed to give them peace.

At first glance there may seem to be another choice of exotic religion on the part of haoles who enjoy telling, with more or less awe, stories based on remnants of Polynesian belief. *Kamaaina* (old-timers) love to tell such stories to *malihini* (newcomers). Clifford Gessler's book, *Hawaii: Isles of Enchantment* has a whole chapter of them. Mrs. Antoinette Withington's *Hawaiian Tapestry* has another.

On closer examination, the subject matter of most of these stories is seen to be of little importance in the lives of those who tell them. It does not matter much to haoles whether ghostly drums are heard on the nights of Kane or not; whether lights gleam at mysterious times and places; whether shadowy figures pass before the eyes of the few who can see them.

Another class of these stories might have practical importance—those that deal in evil omens, such as a curse awaiting people who build on an old burial ground. But such stories do not keep haoles from building. There was one about a real estate development on the slopes of Diamond Head. It is all built up now. There was another about the site of the Royal Hawaiian Hotel at Waikiki. But the hotel stands and prospers.

There was much talk in this vein about the former name of one of the Matson liners, *Malolo*. The literal meaning is "flying fish," but *lolo* may also mean paralysis, or insanity, or "to deride for some misfortune or ill-luck." A *kahuna* (wizard) was hired to take off the curse of the name, and there are elaborations about that, too. Gessler tells one version in full. Eventually the ship was renamed *Matsonia*, when an earlier vessel of that name was sold. This is a rare case, in that something was actually done about the dark murmurs. For that matter, the Matson Company in announcing the change of name attributed it to the wish to keep the traditional name *Matsonia* afloat.

All such yarns, when the spirit in which they are told is considered, and the fact that next to nothing is done about them, boil down to no more than ghost stories with a Polynesian flavor. No one has tried to organize a revival of Polynesian religion around them. No one, I am quite sure, spends much time thinking about them, unless he is working them into a book. There is no danger of anyone suffering for such a faith. No one takes it seriously enough for that. Of the very few who still try to get a kahuna to help them out of a difficulty or revenge them on an enemy, hardly any nowadays are haoles. In short, those who enjoy warming over these bits of old belief are not sharing in Polynesian religion. They are only playing. There may be a dash of romantic feeling in their play, but no more than that.

The lives of traders, planters, businessmen, from the beginning, have been motivated largely by ambition to make money in a strictly haole way. No renunciation of haole prestige there! The missionaries, too, were, *ex officio*, salesmen of haole culture; not only in religion, but in everything except what they regarded as sin. Their official instructions * said, "You are to aim at nothing short of covering those islands with fruitful fields and pleasant dwellings, and schools and churches." A more detailed list of what they were to do for the Hawaiians, in the same document, included the following: "to turn them from their barbarous courses and habits; to introduce, and get into extended operation and influence among them, the arts and institutions and usages of civilized life and society." The rejoicing of Reverend Lorenzo Lyons over signs of a change in table manners shows a complacent assumption of haole superiority that may be typical, though here flippantly expressed. Commenting on a temperance revival at Waimea, Hawaii, in 1847, he said: "A far greater number were seated at tables at these festivals than on any preceding occasion of this kind. What is deserving of particular attention is, these tables are not to disappear at the end of the feast and the guests return to the floor as formerly, but the eating at tables is to be a permanent thing. So there is a little hope yet of Hawaiians becoming civilized."

A good many practical details of Hawaiian living were adopted by haoles, even missionaries, through at least half of the nineteenth century. Missionary borrowings can be pretty well itemized from Reverend Sereno Bishop's reminiscences. As to food: "I think we always had enough food to eat, such as sweet potatoes, taro, poi, goats' milk, bananas, sugar cane, fresh pork, chickens, turkeys, and fish." Of this list, only goats' milk and turkeys were not on the ancient Hawaiian bill of fare. As

* *Instructions of the Prudential Committee of the American Board of Commissioners for Foreign Missions to the Sandwich Islands Mission* (Lahainaluna, 1838).

to dwellings, a house of New England type was pre-fabricated and shipped around the Horn only a year after the arrival of the first missionary band. But such houses were never produced in quantity. Bishop says of his childhood in the 1830's: "Honolulu was a hard-looking old camp in those days. . . . Most of the dwellings were native thatched houses, chiefly pili-grass. . . . When I returned to Honolulu in 1853, after an absence of thirteen years, I was struck by many changes. . . . The major portion of the residents of Honolulu, however, still lived in thatched houses."

When it came to clothing, the missionaries could not go native as the sailor James Coleman had done. Their haole sense of modesty would not permit. So, to quote Bishop again: "Our parents were simply clothed in garments of light material, black being mostly reserved for Sunday. I think their cheaper garments were nearly all cut and sewed by their wives, and could not have been very stylish." Still, they were cut and sewed, a technique foreign to Polynesian culture.

The same value—modesty—militated against use of the Hawaiian language. To quote Bishop again:

We children were not permitted to learn any of the native tongue until later years. The reason of this was to prevent mental contamination. There was no reserve whatever upon any subject in the presence of children in the social and domestic conversation of the native people. The vilest topics were freely discussed in their presence and the children grew up in an atmosphere of the grossest impurity. The same strict tabu was enforced in nearly all the mission families.

But of course the missionaries had to make use of the Hawaiian language in their teaching.

Such early haole borrowings, dictated by utility, dwindled as haole goods and devices became available. Yet there is still enough borrowing by haoles from other cultures to be worth itemizing, for the sake of finding out what values are involved.

The most conspicuous borrowing from Hawaiian culture nowadays is the lei or garland; most commonly of flowers, sometimes of shells or small, bright-colored or fragrant fruits like pandanus and *mokihana*. Men, if they wear hats at all, may affect a feather lei as a hatband, a faint echo of the feather garments of high chiefs in old Hawaii. But the Hawaiian birds whose bright feathers were used for capes or helmets are nearly all extinct. Feathers used for hatbands now are from foreign birds— peacock, turkey, pheasant.

With the use of the flower lei, a little of Polynesian custom has been taken over. Such a lei, as a gift to an arriving or departing friend, is almost obligatory in Hawaii. It is also appropriate as a gift to the guest of honor at any party, or among women for ornament on any festive occasion. To be sure, its uses do not differ greatly from the uses of cut flowers in haole cities. Moreover, this borrowing from Hawaiian culture has been commercialized after the haole pattern. A considerable number of Hawaiians get their living by making and selling leis. Yet the use of the lei still involves a remnant of Polynesian symbolism of good will. Even a touch of Polynesian kindliness may have carried over into haole life with it.

The tides of fashion characteristic of women's clothing in haole culture also bring in and out with them occasional borrowings from Oriental costume. For a while, richly embroidered Chinese mandarin coats were quite the best thing for evening wraps. At another time, Japanese silk *haori* coats were in favor for the same use. Chinese pajamas similarly "came in" and "went out" for wearing about the house. At the beach, Japanese workmen's jackets (*hapi*) were much worn at one time as wraps over bathing suits. At another, Japanese *geta* (clogs) or *tabi* (socks; more precisely, foot mittens) have been popular to keep sand from between the toes. Rather more constant seems to be a fondness for jade and other Chinese jewelry among haole women.

In architecture the story is much the same. The only strictly Hawaiian thatched house in the islands is a reconstructed one in the Bishop Museum. I know of no house in strictly Chinese style, and only one purely Japanese—that which Dr. Robert Faus imported and set up at his place near Koko Head. But the line of many a roof suggests the old thatched houses; here and there an eave upturned at the corners, an ornamentally shaped gate or window, or a bit of staggered latticework, is reminiscent of China; while an occasional sliding wall, stone lantern, or bit of landscaping recalls Japan.

Inside haole houses, borrowings from other cultures are more conspicuous. Polynesian Hawaii has contributed the *lauhala* (pandanus) mat for floor covering, or for various little articles of haole design, from waste baskets to napkin rings. Especially in older houses, *punee* or *hikiee*—large low beds adapted from the old Hawaiian bed of piled mats—are used for lounging as well as sleeping. Stone poi pounders, though they no longer pound poi, may serve as door stops and ornaments. Wooden bowls are another bit of Hawaiian decoration. Now that the old hand-hewn bowls have become rare, lathe-turned bowls or modern specimens carved in the shape of leaves, may be substituted. In the same way, China has contributed furniture of teak or bamboo; porcelain, cloisonné, brassware, silk scrolls, and embroidered pieces. Some of these articles—chinaware, silk, and furniture such as *tansu* (a kind of chiffonier)—may also come from Japan; which also enriches the mixture with colored prints, lacquerware, and innumerable delicately made little gadgets.

In food the picture is still fundamentally the same. Only a few foodstuffs have been adopted and retained purely for utility. It seems to take time to acquire a taste for poi, the taro porridge which was the Hawaiian staple. Yet a fair number of haoles are still fond of it. Haole children are sometimes raised on it, since it is supposed to be healthful. If they begin young enough, they seem to take to poi enthusiastically. Haoles in Hawaii eat much more rice, too, than in the United States. They have learned to cook it in the Oriental way, which is incomparably more appetizing than the soggy stuff produced in American mainland kitchens. And some Chinese vegetables, readily grown in Hawaii, appear often on haole tables.

But the most conspicuous borrowing in food is a feast in the style of some nonhaole culture. A Hawaiian luau is one of the indispensable forms of "good time" that newcomers are taught to seek in Hawaii. And the more Hawaiian it is the better. There, even the beginner must try to eat poi with his fingers, along with the other Hawaiian delicacies cooked in the earth oven: pork, sweet potatoes, fish, chicken, young taro leaves in coconut cream, various coconut puddings, edible seaweed, even (though with squirms and giggles) stewed octopus.

Nowadays, though, nearly all luau are served on tables.

A similar festivity is a Chinese dinner. A common name for it is "chop suey dinner," though the menu may or may not include chop suey, said to have been improvised in the United States by a Chinese cook. The most popular kind of Japanese feast emphasizes a similar hybrid, *hekka* or *sukiyaki*. This is said to have been devised by Dutch traders in the days when they alone were permitted to visit Japan. If so, the object evidently was to get away from the strict vegetarianism required of Buddhists; for this dish, in addition to such Oriental ingredients as soy bean curd and bamboo sprouts, includes beef or chicken.

Sports are another center of borrowing by haoles. The regular regime for tourists—those active enough to enjoy it—includes riding the surf at Waikiki, either on a surfboard or in an outrigger canoe. Distinguished visitors may be regaled with the spectacle of a *hukilau*. This is a Hawaiian form of beach fishing. The fish are surrounded by a long cord held up with floats and tufted with leaves. The cord is gradually pulled in, narrowing the circle and herding in the fish, frightened by the writhing leaves, until they can be speared or scooped up in hand nets. A few hardy haoles, mostly hikers of the Trail and Mountain Club, have enjoyed another old Hawaiian sport—sliding down steep grassy slopes on sleds made of tufts of *ti* leaves.

The Orient, too, has made its contribution to sport, though a less popular one. In borrowing from the Chinese, haoles of Hawaii seem to have done little more than follow recurrent American fads for some Chinese game. Once upon a time it was fan-tan; something like a generation later, mah-jongg. But children in Hawaii, no matter of what ancestry, play what is said to be a Chinese form of a widespread finger-matching game. They call it "junk an' a po," said to be a corruption of a Chinese name. The game itself differs hardly at all from the haole version, wherein scissors cut paper, paper covers stone, stone blunts scissors. (There is also a Japanese version, *ken*, in which geisha girls are trained. A Polynesian version is played in some of the southern islands, but I find no record of its having reached Hawaii.)

Fewer, but more constant, have been the haole devotees of Japanese athletics. Greatest interest has been taken in judo, sporting form of the old jiujitsu, with the more deadly holds and tricks left out. Smaller numbers have gone in for sumo wrestling, *kendo* fencing with bamboo foils, and a very few for *kyudo*, Japanese archery.

This summarizes haole borrowings from other cultures. If some details have been overlooked, they probably do not differ in kind from those mentioned. Nearly all can be brought under the two main headings of adornment and recreation. In other words, they are essentially play, with novelty the main value behind the choice of these particular forms of play. The more extensive borrowings of earlier days, motivated by utility, dwindled when haole wares could be chosen instead. The haole borrowings that remain are little supplements to haole culture rather than substitutions for it. Haole prestige is not threatened by these little borrowings.

Converts to Buddhism are different. So are the few thoroughgoing romantics. So were the early mariners who went native—to the extent that their adoption of Hawaiian ways involved a rejection of anything haole.

These exceptions have been examined with some care for fear of slighting what importance they have. But clearly they are few, and apply only to a few individuals. Questioning haole prestige seriously has never occurred to the vast majority of haoles.

PART II

RELIEF FROM HAOLE DOMINANCE

PART II

Relief from Haole Dominance

TO make life worth living, everybody has to be fairly well pleased with himself and his kind. Human conceit, the world over, ordinarily takes care of that want with the comfortable assumption that I and my kind are the best in the world. The less we know of other kinds of people, the easier it is to feel sure of our own superiority. But in places like Hawaii, where different kinds of people are together all the time, that assumption is put to the test. The outcome there, as we have seen, has been haole prestige; a dogma so generally accepted that people who are not haole can hardly take it for granted that their kind is best. Haoles are best, by decree of public opinion.

Under these conditions, all who are not haole are threatened with a sense of inferiority. The pressure on their feelings is not confined to opinion, attitudes, and similar intangibles. Haole prestige is expressed in action to the extent of affecting the most vital concerns: opportunity to make a living, choice of a place to live, choice of friends. In all these matters, generally speaking, haoles come first. Wherever there is not room for all, those not haole are expected to be content with what is left over. True, discrimination in Hawaii is less severe than in many other places. Nonhaoles have some chance to overcome their handicap. But it is by no means an even chance. Whatever gains they make are made against the current. To save their peace of mind, they must do something to overcome an oppressive conviction of inferiority. The value that motivates what they do will be called relief; relief from the stress of humiliation. How that value has been pursued in Hawaii will be considered in the next three chapters.

The courses that people may take to win relief from stress have been classified by Alexander Leighton, in *The Governing of Men*, under three main heads: Aggression, Withdrawal, and Coöperation. The scheme seems to fit the case of Hawaii. It must be borne in mind that the three are not mutually exclusive. A social movement or individual course of action can represent any combination of them.

VI

Aggression

AGGRESSION here means any hostile act, including speech. Since it is regarded as a response to stress, it involves no judgment as to "Who started it?" "Counteraggression" would fit the case more exactly; but "aggression" is simpler, and in general use. What follows is an attempt to assess the relative importance of aggression, in this sense, as a means of seeking relief from haole dominance.

Overt, concerted aggression between Hawaiians and haoles was common during early contacts, as already noted. But this was not a response to haole dominance, for haoles were not yet dominant. These fights were an early stage in the process by which they became so.

Indirectly, haole influence contributed to a battle between Hawaiian chiefs in 1819. Kamehameha, shortly before his death in that year, had told the chiefs that he wished to have his son Liholiho succeed him as ruler of the islands. At the same time he bequeathed his celebrated war god, Ku-kailimoku, to his nephew Kekuaokalani. The god was represented by a carved wooden figure with yellow feather headdress. When Liholiho, as Kamehameha II, publicly abolished the tabu system by eating with women, and ordered the destruction of sacred enclosures and images of the gods, Kekuaokalani led the adherents of the old faith in open revolt. He was killed and his followers defeated in the battle of Kuamoo.

It seems likely that Kekuaokalani had hoped to be chosen himself as Kamehameha's successor. In that case he was moved to aggression partly by the stress of humiliation. Again, there is no doubt that abolition of the tabus and destruction of sacred objects were due ultimately to haole influence. So in rising to the defense of the god entrusted to him, and of old beliefs in general, Kekuaokalani was in a sense taking aggressive action against haole encroachment. Still, haole influence affected him only indirectly. It was not haole prestige that brought humiliation upon him. That did not yet seriously threaten a high chief's self-esteem. So this, again, is not aggression of the kind we are after.

In the following year (1820) Liholiho became panicky over reports of impending revolution and foreign, particularly American, designs upon the islands. He ordered a general deportation of foreigners with the exception of those attached to him or to his minister Kalanimoku. However, this seems to have been mainly an anti-American move. One contemporary source attributes it to agitation by two British residents.* At any rate, it is no clear case of aggression against haoles in general. Haole prestige, at least to the extent of fearing haole arms, does show in the king's nervousness. This act may represent aggression against haole prestige in some formative state, but no more than that. At any rate, the attempt to carry out the deportation order was halfhearted and shortlived.

When Kauikeaouli became Kamehameha III in 1825, he was only 12 years old. So Kaahumanu governed as

* H. W. Bradley, *The American Frontier in Hawaii* (Stanford University, Palo Alto, 1942).

regent until her death in 1832. She was an outstanding devotee of the American mission, and hers was a Calvinist rule. Her successor Kinau, daughter of Kamehameha and half-sister of the young king, was also a follower of the mission. But she had neither Kaahumanu's strength of character nor her experience in government. Besides, by this time the king was getting tired of leaving his power in the hands of women. His rebellion took the form of indulgence in revelry abhorred by the mission. His example was rather generally followed by the people. Drunkenness and gambling came into fashion. So did a number of old native recreations which the mission had tried to suppress. Reverend Levi Chamberlain complained: "The sound of the hula is beginning again to rend the air; persons are seen venturing forth to roll the *maika* stone." This clearly involved aggression in response to stress. Moreover it went beyond an individual revolt of king against regent. Yet still the aggression was not against haole domination in general; for whoever opposed the mission in those days did so with the approval, and often at the instigation, of the antimission faction among haoles.

Resentment of haole infiltration is particularly apparent during the 1840's. A petition to Kamehameha III in 1845, asking that foreigners be dismissed from office in the kingdom and prohibited from acquiring land, is the most conspicuous example. It was signed by 1,600 Hawaiians from the island of Maui. The king appointed a commission of three to look into the matter: John Ricord, one of the very foreigners against whom the complaint was directed; John Young, half-Hawaiian son of the first Kamehameha's famous adviser; and John Ii, a prominent Hawaiian supporter of the mission. It is not surprising that they took the protest lightly. They found "that although there appears to be some feeling among the natives of Maui growing from a misapprehension of Your Majesty's policy in naturalizing foreigners and in calling upon them to assist in the duties of your Government, and although that feeling seems to have been engendered by some unseen foreign Agent, yet that the Agent thus at work seems to have been able to elude detection."

The reply of the petitioners (or the unseen foreign Agent), even if unfair to some prominent haoles, was an eloquent, partly prophetic statement of Hawaiian grievances. Witness these excerpts:

It is not to benefit this people, but for their own personal interests that foreigners suddenly take the oath of allegiance to this government. . . . Those who want a building spot, or a large piece of land for themselves; those who wish to become chiefs, or head men upon the lands, and those who wish to marry wives immediately. . . . Do they desire the people to become enlightened? It is not clear to us that they do. . . . If any one of us become assistants of the Chiefs, his pay for the most part is in goods; the most of the dollars are for foreign chiefs. . . .

What is to be the result of so many foreigners taking the oath of allegiance? This is it, in our opinion; this kingdom will pass into their hands, and that too very soon. Foreigners come on shore with cash, ready to purchase land; but we have not the means to purchase lands. . . . If we had not been loitering around after our chiefs, thinking to accustom ourselves to that mode of life, then perhaps we should be prepared to compete with foreigners. . . . Foreigners will say to us, perhaps, purchase according to your ability to purchase and husband well. Very well; but why are we poor at this time? Because we have been subject to the ancient laws till within these few years. . . .

Our King and Sovereign Kamehameha, have compassion upon us. . . . If the introduction of foreigners into this kingdom could be deferred for ten years perhaps, and we could have places given us suitable for cultivation and pasturing cattle, by that time some of our embarrassments might be removed, and it might be proper to introduce foreigners into the kingdom. But if many foreigners are introduced into the kingdom at this time, this will be our end; we shall become the servants of foreigners.

Here at last aggression against haole dominance, though in the mild form of verbal protest and appeal for aid, is unmistakable.

Whaling in the Pacific reached its height about the same time. The seasonal influx of carousing sailors inevitably led to occasional brawls with Hawaiians. How far these involved aggression against haole prestige it is impossible to make out. But at least a newspaper comment of the time suggests the presence of such a feeling. *The Polynesian* of October 10, 1846, discussing a fight between Hawaiians and sailors from a British ship, said: "The natives have enough of disregard of life and savage passions among them, to be not at all backward in taking part in an affray, especially when the cry is 'haole' against 'kanaka.' "

When Reverend and Mrs. Amos Cooke opened a Chiefs' Children's School in 1839, they had a hard time managing young chiefs who had been accustomed to indulging every whim. With the best of intentions, the two missionaries applied the strict methods by which they themselves had been brought up. Mrs. Cooke wrote: "We are obliged to discipline them, sometimes by shutting them in a room by themselves, sometimes by inflicting pain. . . . The Sabbath is a trying day to us. The children feel some as I recollect to have felt when young —the deprivation of accustomed amusement." When one of the boys became sick with fright at having stepped over a mark in the road which his companion attributed to a sorcerer, "Mr. Cooke told the children that they must go out no more to walk till they were not afraid of marks, for there were many of them about. Mischievous children would mark; indeed, he had often made marks himself. We kept them in about a fortnight, when they declared themselves freed of their fears and obtained more liberty." After one escapade in which "the boys and girls came very near getting together," Mrs. Cooke wrote: "We have drawn all our cords much tighter. They squirm some."

For a while this treatment seemed to work. "We find to our joy and satisfaction that the restraints which we are throwing around the children do not operate unfavorably by making them wish to forsake us." But the German sea captain, Steen Bille, who visited the school about 1845, saw a side of the matter that the missionaries missed:

They also entertained us with one of the teetotalistic drinking songs, praising the water and beginning with these words: "Nothing is so good for the youthful blood as clear sparkling water." It seemed to be their favorite song and the whole school joined in a very strong chorus. I could not help but ask Prince Moses, a big square built boy, when we were alone, if he did not prefer to sing "sparkling champagne," and he confessed quite frankly that I was right, but asked me for Heaven's sake not to speak about it.

Prince Moses was not able to conceal his wicked proclivities from his teachers much longer before he was expelled from the school. He had been caught in a clandestine affair with the queen.

When graduates of the school came into power in government, they generally turned against the American mission. Of Alexander Liholiho and Lot Kamehameha, both of whom became kings, Mrs. Cooke wrote in 1846 (mixing her metaphors badly): "I tremble to see them enter on the stage of action with uncircumcised hearts. But they seem hardened on religious subjects. They are more like New England hardened sinners than like Hawaiians." Alexander, when he became Kamehameha IV, and his wife Emma, another former pupil of the Chiefs' Children's School, favored the Church of England rather than the American church. Kamehameha IV curtailed missionary influence in government. Lot, when he became Kamehameha V, seemed on the whole more friendly to the evangelistic mission. Yet during his reign a number of measures of which the mission could not approve went into effect; for one, the licensing of native healers, who relied in part upon ancient magic. Most outspoken of all in opposition to the missionaries was David Kalakaua, when he became king. But since he also exemplifies responses other than aggression, his acts will be analyzed later. Here it is enough to note that in all these instances aggression was not directed against haole prestige but only against the particular institution that had imposed haole standards in extreme form, and imposed them with grim severity.

During Kalakaua's reign and that of his successor Queen Liliuokalani—that is to say, during the dying days of the monarchy—general Hawaiian resentment of haole domination surged up again. As early as 1880, antihaole sentiment was expressed in an election manifesto by Moreno, who for five days in August held the office of premier. Advocating reservation of all public offices for Hawaiians, he said the thing to do was "to throw out these foreigners and to elevate to high positions the people to whom belongs the country, i.e., the red-skins."

Of Hawaiian feeling in the 1890's, Reverend Samuel Damon said: "The Hawaiians had grown to a feeling of independence, and in company with the queen they wanted to throw off that Anglo-Saxon domination which has been with them and controlled them all these years. . . . It is the clashing of two nationalities for supremacy." After her deposition, the queen and her supporters secretly collected arms. In 1895 there was an open outbreak aimed at restoring her to the throne. Though the revolt was not well enough organized to give the provisional republic much trouble, it was the climax of a series of events that clearly show concerted aggression in response to haole encroachment.

After that, aggression conspicuous enough to get on record has been confined to individuals or, at most, small groups. The most spectacular instance is that celebrated in Jack London's story, "Koolau the Leper." When victims of leprosy were first isolated in the settlement at Kalaupapa, Molokai, this man, a Hawaiian cowboy, resisted the quarantine order. The disease had not gone far enough to disable him. He took refuge on a nearly inaccessible ridge in the isolated valley of Kalalau, Kauai.

When the deputy sheriff, who had been his friend, came after him, the leper drew a deadline and warned him not to cross. The sheriff crossed and was shot dead. Later the leper fought it out with a company of soldiers. He escaped, but was wounded, and later found dead. His aggression, of course, was only against enforcement of the particular decree that threatened his liberty. Yet without general haole dominance the issue could never have come up.

The most spectacular case of the years just before Pearl Harbor involved several young men whose names indicated Hawaiian as well as Oriental and, for that matter, haole ancestry. It was the subject of voluminous printed accounts, particularly in newspapers. But it is very difficult to analyze. An apt summary is that of the psychologist Porteus in his book *Calabashes and Kings: an Introduction to Hawaii:*

Accusations of a brutal sex assault were brought by a white woman, a "navy wife," against a group of island youths of mixed racial origins. Then followed a punitive murder and the reverberations of this case were heard all over America. The picture of the islands presented by much of the mainland press at that time was hardly that of a paradise but rather of a dark jungle where white women were unsafe. The case presented so many unusual features, and the credibility of the complainant was so much in question that island opinion was acutely divided.

Exactly what happened and how, let alone what motives were involved, is still far from clear. Aggression against haole dominance may have underlain whatever crime these young men committed. But the case is clouded by motives irrelevant to this inquiry. The "angling" of the account in mainland newspapers as something bordering on insurrection by ill-disciplined "natives" was vehemently supported, perhaps suggested, by the admiral in command of the Hawaii naval district at the time. Some naval officers, with whom Hawaii's strategic importance naturally outweighed other considerations, seem to have used the revolting nature of the case as an argument for increased military control over the islands. The anti-Oriental feeling of the Pacific states, as expressed in newspapers such as those controlled by Hearst, found a welcome outlet in this view of the case.

The suggestion that the islands had become unsafe for white women can be judged by a glimpse at some of the unquestioned circumstances of the case. A young white woman in evening clothes, not cold sober, walked alone, late at night, along a little-frequented road not far from the Honolulu waterfront. Regardless of other factors that are open to question, in what seaport of the world would a woman be safe from hoodlums under those conditions? Our only conclusion must be that if aggression against haole dominance was involved—as it may have been—it was only one of a welter of motives.

Similarly, aggression as an outlet to pressure from haole dominance may have been one of the elements in little brawls between Hawaiian youths and service men, that were not uncommon at Waikiki during the 1930's; also presumably before and since. These differ little from fights between youthful gangs or factions in mainland cities, in which none but haoles are involved. Yet other group or class distinctions probably operate there in a similar way. Further, it is not unlikely that the motivation of a number of crimes and criminal careers may include this factor. The only way to make sure would be a thorough study of individual cases.

One minimal form of aggression remains to be considered; the usual solace of underdogs, that of grumbling among themselves. It is my impression that this is not uncommon among Hawaiians whenever latent resentment of haole dominance is irritated in any way. But such an impression is next to impossible to verify. Grumbling is one of the most evanescent forms of behavior. And Hawaiians generally retain enough Polynesian politeness to abstain from antihaole grumbling in the presence of a haole. Political campaign speeches in Hawaii occasionally take the form of an appeal to the underdog by grumbling against the wealthy, who are mostly haoles. But as this is a standard technique of American politicians, it cannot be relied upon as evidence of anything specifically Hawaiian.

A little experience of my own will have to do, for illustration of a response I consider fairly common, without being able to prove it. In the course of a vacation spent in driving and camping about the island of Hawaii, my wife and I stayed for two days at Kalapana, then the end of the surfaced road in the rather out-of-the-way Puna district. An old Hawaiian who lived near the beach where we pitched our tent showed us through a cave, whose entrance was remarkably well concealed, and which he said had been a place of refuge in the old days. I was uncertain whether his volunteering to be our guide was a case of old-fashioned Polynesian hospitality, in which case I did not want to insult him by offering money; or whether he was acculturated enough to cut in on the tourist trade. Unable to make up my mind, I watched for indications, but did nothing at the time.

The indication came next day, while we were breaking camp. The old fellow sat watching us with his son-in-law, who had gone with us through the cave. Confident that we could not understand Hawaiian, he poured out his indignation in a stream of talk in which the word "haole" recurred often, with bitter emphasis. As nearly as I could make out, he was condemning the whole race for tight-fistedness. At this late moment—a most awkward one, but my last chance—I did offer to pay him for his services of the day before. He took the money with a grumpy air, as much as to say "About time!" Aggression against haole dominance? A little bit, maybe.

Aggression on the part of Chinese immigrants was often turned against themselves at first, to judge by Prince Liholiho's comment on their "considerable disposition to hang themselves." Yet the story of the one who was found casting silver bullets, to shoot a devil that had cut off his cue, shows that they sometimes turned on their tormentors. During the 1880's, when feeling among haoles rather generally turned against them because of their increasing numbers and prosperity, the Chinese responded with a distinct flare-up of violence. The medical student Vernon Briggs noted in his diary in 1881: "Dr. Emerson is very busy. Today he went to the Pauoa valley to investigate a murder by a Chinaman, and also to Waianae, to attend Captain Rose, who was suffering from injuries inflicted by a Chinaman on his sugar plantation, who struck him with a hoe and broke his arm and several ribs."

The lives of the district justice and deputy sheriff were threatened in a riot at Hanalei, Kauai, in 1884. The riot was attributed by the marshal of the kingdom to a Chinese society. In 1889 the royal cabinet, in its report on Chinese infiltration, declared: "Within the past two years there have been three murders by Chinese secret society members. . . . Several persons suspected of giving information to the police have suddenly disappeared, leaving no trace behind." Dr. Clarence Glick, who has made a systematic study of Chinese societies in Hawaii, says some of them originated as "institutions for counter-attack."

Aggression among the Chinese seems to have died out with the hostility that provoked it. The "hatchet-man" and "tong-war" kind of thing, for which mainland Chinatowns were long notorious, never took firm hold in the islands. Police activities involving the Chinese in Hawaii, for at least a generation, have been typically raids on gambling games or opium dens, or tracing down unauthorized immigrants who had been smuggled in by friends or relatives. Rarely have the Chinese been involved in crimes of violence.

The Japanese in Hawaii have been notably law abiding. Their record in this respect is the best in the whole population. Yet under special stress, they, too, have been known to resort to violence. The most spectacular instance was an attack by Japanese field hands at Kahuku plantation upon their Chinese fellow workers in 1899. As in all the cases cited, information is scanty. Nothing is on record about how ill-feeling developed between the two. But when the wrath of the Japanese reached the bursting point, they armed themselves one Sunday morning with whatever came to hand, fell upon the Chinese in their barracks, and in a few minutes killed three men and wounded about 50. They did not resist the police sent out from Honolulu.

Apparently the attack was to some extent planned and organized. The *Commercial Advertiser* reported: "The Japanese were so bold that they had a general. He was a little man mounted on a white horse, and wearing leggings that came above his knees." This is enough to hint at national feeling as one ingredient in the emotional brew. And since the year was 1899, when Japanese resentment over annexation of Hawaii to the United States was at its height, it seems not too farfetched to suggest that resentment against domination by haoles may have been another ingredient. To the extent that this motive was involved, aggression aroused by haoles was displaced; that is, redirected against the Chinese as a more accessible and vulnerable target.

The generally peaceable character of the Japanese population was illustrated by two long and serious strikes on the sugar plantations, particularly those of the island of Oahu. During what is still recalled as "the Japanese strike" of 1909, in spite of evictions and arrests that now seem highhanded, there was little or no counterviolence on the part of the strikers. Associated with a later strike, in 1920, there was one conspicuous case—the dynamiting of a house at Olaa on the island of Hawaii. For this, 15 Japanese labor leaders were convicted of conspiracy. The house was that of J. Sakamaki, said to have been active in opposition to the strike. Here again, if aggression against haoles underlay this act, it was displaced, and redirected against a fellow Japanese. The strikes themselves can be regarded as aggression in the sense used here. But, as in other cases, it was only against the particular application of haole dominance that affected the strikers directly.

The only account of an individual case that brings out motives at all clearly is that of a boy of Japanese parentage whose aggression took the form of a particularly atrocious crime. In 1928, at the age of 19, he kidnaped and murdered a much younger haole boy. He sent a fantastically worded ransom note to the boy's father and, after the killing, got money from him. After a period of public excitement, intensified by a lurid, vainglorious note sent to a newspaper, and by the finding of the murdered boy's body, he was arrested, tried, convicted, and sentenced to death.

During the interval before execution of the sentence, Lockwood Myrick, Jr., then a teacher of philosophy at the University of Hawaii, sent an open letter to the governor of the territory, asking for commutation of the sentence on the ground that the killer was insane in the legal sense of the term. It did not succeed in preventing execution of the sentence.

Looking over Myrick's letter now for evidence of aggression in response to haole prestige, it seems a remarkable case history: carefully documented, penetrating, and for the most part convincing. Myrick speaks of "my twenty years and more of first-hand, inside experience with insanity and my training in detecting, analyzing and removing the complexes of the insane." Nothing more is available about these qualifications. His own emotional involvement is unmistakable. At one point he says "Only those of us who are more or less like him can imagine his state of utter helplessness." Whether in spite of this involvement or because of it, the document is incomparable for the purpose here in view. What follows is a summary of relevant evidence. Quotations are all from the culprit's statements, but the analysis follows that of Myrick.

The murderer will be called by his first name, Myles. It is one of those haole names common among children of Oriental immigrants. Nothing is on record as to how he got it, but he may well have chosen it himself, as many nisei children do. At any rate, the archaic character of the name and its spelling suggest the romantic, naïvely literary bent which is characteristic of him.

Myles was born in the plantation town of Waialua on Oahu, but spent his later boyhood in Honolulu. He was small and slight, and seems to have suffered from a sense of physical inferiority. His mother told Myrick that when he first went to school he made a good impression. But later—just how much later is uncertain—he got into unspecified difficulties, and was repeatedly whipped by one or more teachers. When he was in the fourth grade he became so reluctant to stay in school that his mother, who had never inflicted bodily punishment before, could only get him to attend by adding whippings at home to those received in school. This experience is said to have instilled in him a fear of other people. Certainly throughout his boyhood he kept much to himself, made few friends, lived more in his own imagination than most children. He was devoted to books and—later on, at least—to motion pictures. So far his response to stress is one of withdrawal.

To this he added, in one respect, a response of coöperation. Unable to excel in boyish activities among playmates, he tried to make up for it by excelling in school. In this he succeeded to the extent of graduating from grammar school at the head of his class. That rare experience of success, together with the solitary life that gave little opportunity for testing his abilities against those of playmates, seems to have given him an exaggerated opinion of his own intellectual ability. In psychological tests administered after the crime he was rated low in planning and analysis. But he had the qualities needed for success in the classroom: fairly quick capacity to learn, retentive memory, and steady application.

As we have seen among nisei in general, nearly all his environment instilled in him the ambition to succeed in an American way. As the oldest son among seven children, he was strengthened in this by Japanese tradition, with its emphasis on obligation to parents and family. Clearly, the way open to success for him was to develop his special abilities by continuing in school. But the family income would not permit. His father was earning $45 a month; his sister, about $24 ($5.50 a week). Rent came to $20 a month. An income of less than $740 a year would not support a family of nine in Honolulu, even by the meagerest standards. Myles had to quit school, thus closing the way to American success. For him it was a major frustration. In his confession he said: "That was my biggest disappointment. I wanted to study." And again "I wanted education so very much."

He got a job as attendant or orderly in a hospital, working 12 hours a day for $45 a month. There was little satisfaction to be got from the work, and the long hours must have been dreary. Out of his $45 a month, he contributed $40 to the support of the family. After a year or more at the hospital, he asked for a raise of $5 a month, to bring his wages up to those of another boy there. He was told to wait another six months. At the end of that time he asked again, and got the same answer.

In this plight most of his strongest impulses were thwarted. Quitting school had meant, as Myrick puts it, "that his was to be a life of inferiority." His job was not rewarding in itself, and the $5 a month he kept out of his wages did not allow him the pleasure of spending freely. "I never had much clothing in my life." One haole way out of so bleak a situation might have been to take to drink; a Chinese way (recent Chinese), to take to opium. Myles had just one vice, masturbation, and it did the opposite of helping him. Whatever relief it gave was more than offset by shame, and by the fear, from what he heard about ill effects of the practice, that it would increase his physical weakness. He had not the solace of friendship, though he does mention correspondence with girls. "You see, it's funny about me. I couldn't make many friends. I rather be alone with books. They are my only friends. Most of my life was spent with books, magazines. Reading." The unreal life of paper and films was the only solace he had. It was not enough.

As a last resort, Myles took a Japanese way out of a situation that seemed to him hopeless. He quit his job at the hospital with the intention of committing suicide. This is the first appearance of the desperate response of aggression, and the aggression was first directed against himself. What means he took is not stated. At any rate, the attempt at suicide failed. He succeeded only in doing himself enough damage to keep him at home for a while, convalescing.

During this interval, when despondency, weakness,

and helplessness were at their height, he suffered another humiliation. A collector for the trust company that acted as agent for the house in which they were living called to get the rent. Lacking Myles' salary, there was not enough money to pay. They begged the collector to wait, but he threatened to have them evicted. Myles' mother cried. His father was shamed. He felt that he had failed in his duty toward them. This seems to have been the final blow that turned the impulse to aggression, already awakened, against those he blamed for humiliating his family.

He began to plan the murder. He chose as victim an officer of the trust company at whom he could strike through his small son. There was no personal hatred; in fact, he considered the president of the company but "could not go against him because I know him."

The motives, partly stated in his confession and partly brought out by Myrick's analysis, were these:

To get enough money, for ransom, to send his parents to Japan. "As for my part, I don't know, but only I wanted to sacrifice myself so I could bring happiness to my parents."

To prove himself powerful and successful by an exploit of an American kind. He copied his plan mainly from an account, found at the public library, of the Loeb and Leopold kidnaping and murder in Chicago, four years earlier. Some details were taken from reports of other sensational cases.

To express his impulse fully and freely and feel, for once, a sense of power; partly from the prominence the crime would give him, partly from the pleasure of spending money freely. As to the prominence, his letter to the

Star-Bulletin begins: "As a result of our recent exploits, we 'Three Kings' find the community all agog . . ." As to the pleasure of spending, "I bought a first-class ticket to town. It makes one feel good to spend money as freely as you wanted; to have the best of things; instead of second-class, go first-class ticket."

To give himself up and die. This seems to have been his intention from the first. "I have to pay for this." He seems to have thought of his death as paying, not only for the crime but in some way for the ransom money. "If I returned the boy safely to Mr. —— and he got the boy, some of the story would leak out and in my mind, I thought I got the money just like stealing. I always would have been branded as a thief. I rather kill the boy and die myself."

Further details of Myrick's analysis, especially his interpretation of the fantastic symbolism in the ransom note, the *Star-Bulletin* letter, and a scenario in which a phantasmagoric version of the crime is outlined as a motion-picture plot, are revealing psychologically. But they are not necessary here. The case as outlined is adequate to illustrate the response of aggression. Plainly the sense of inferiority was too strong to bear. Plainly, too, haole domination, especially as expressed in economic status, played a part in the stress under which the boy finally broke. Yet the source of stress was not envisioned as haole prestige. And when hostility finally surged up, it was not directed against haoles as such, but first against himself, and finally against the particular agency that dealt the last blow. Haole prestige remained unshaken in his mind. Even when his goal of success took a fantastic form repugnant to the standards of any human society, it still followed an American pattern.

The attack on Pearl Harbor touched off a veritable eruption of rumors about anti-American aggression on the part of Japanese or nisei residents. Nearly all of these stories turned out to be untrue. The evidence is convincingly presented by Lind in *Hawaii's Japanese*. One case, though, seems beyond question: the widely publicized "Niihau incident."

At the time of the Japanese attack, the population of the little island of Niihau, off the coast of Kauai, numbered less than 200. All but two were Hawaiian or part-Hawaiian. These two were of Japanese descent: Sinichi Shintani, born in Japan, and Yoshio Harada, Hawaiian-born nisei. Niihau was extremely isolated, partly as a matter of policy on the part of the owners, who tried to preserve there the kind of life that Hawaiians had lived in an earlier day. There was no radio or outside wire communication. So Niihau knew nothing of the attack on Pearl Harbor until, several hours after it had begun, a Japanese plane crash-landed there.

The pilot, who had been stunned at first but not badly hurt, talked to Shintani and Harada, the only ones on the island who could understand him. Whether by threats or promises, or by assuring them that Japan was about to take over the islands anyway, he induced them to help him in an attempt to add Niihau to Japan's conquests.

For several days the three carried on a reign of terror. Some of the Hawaiians on the island hid, some were captured. A few succeeded in getting over the ridge of the island to where a whaleboat was kept, and rowing it to

Kauai. But before they returned with troops, the pilot had threatened and then shot Benjamin Kanahele, who, at the point of the pilot's gun, had been pretending to help in a search for another Hawaiian. Kanahele, unarmed and wounded, turned upon the Japanese and, with some help from his wife, killed him, suffering three wounds before it was over.

Harada was there, armed with a shotgun. But instead of shooting Kanahele, he turned the gun upon himself.

Here is aggression, beyond a doubt. Though the immediate victims were Hawaiians, it amounted to taking arms against the United States. In evaluating this instance as a sample of nisei behavior, three points must be kept in mind. First, it is the only case of the kind. Second, the circumstances were fantastically exceptional. As to what would have happened if the Japanese had taken the islands, we can only wonder. Doubtless there would have been collaborators, as in the countries occupied by Germany; but for that matter, doubtless there would have been some haoles among them; as there were, it is said, American collaborators with Germany in France. And finally, one of the aggressors—the nisei one—seems to have repented at the last moment. At any rate, he turned his aggression against himself. As if to complete the expiation, one of his relatives also committed suicide later on, on Kauai.

Finally, a glance at aggression in the form of talk, which has been suggested as not uncommon among Hawaiians. Everybody who was in the islands before the war heard at least one story about a Japanese maid who told her haole employers that in case of war she would side with Japan. No doubt such answers have been made to questions on the subject. But was not such a question itself aggressive? Would not such inquiries, of themselves, build up counteraggression? What is more, so consistent a pattern runs through the many versions of this story as to suggest that it was passing into folklore.

"Baron Hee Hee" and "Baroness Tee Hee," who broadcast in English over Radio Tokyo during the war, are said to have been a former instructor at the University of Hawaii and a girl born on the island of Maui. In Hawaii itself, Lind gives several well-attested examples of aggressive talk by nisei, some of them apparently cases of *in vino veritas*. Clearly, aggressive talk was commoner than aggressive action. But that does not make it common. As compared with the coöperative behavior recounted by Lind, and illustrated here in the chapter on Coöperation, aggressive talk by nisei seems to have been comparatively rare. What there was of it was still a harmless outlet for the emotional pressure inevitable under the circumstances.

Throughout this inquiry into aggression in response to haole prestige, the intention has been to make the most of all available evidence, in order not to slight what importance it may have. The result has included a good deal of groping amid uncontrolled factors, some of which were doubtless not even recognized. Evidence of the kind sought turned out to be scanty; and much of what there was, of dubious significance. Nearly always there were complications—specific sources of stress more immediate and obvious than the general pressure of haole dominance.

This accumulation of hints does seem enough to prove that aggression has been one response to haole dominance right along. More cogently, though, the very weakness of the case proves that, except in one or two crises, aggression has not been the predominant response but a distinctly exceptional one. The only form in which it may be common is the mildest form possible, that of taking it out in talk.

VII

Withdrawal

MANY and devious are the ways of withdrawing from an intolerable situation. Not all of those that may spring from contact of cultures in Hawaii can be explored here. For example, several forms of insanity are ways of withdrawal. Beaglehole, in an appendix to *Some Modern Hawaiians*, reviews figures on psychosis in Hawaii, classified by race, and suggests the presence of cultural factors. But analysis of possible withdrawal from haole dominance into psychosis would be a large undertaking in itself. That is one of the lines of inquiry not attempted. Another is withdrawal into religious seclusion. That too would require deeper study of individual cases than seems feasible in a work as broad in scope as this. Withdrawal into religion will be considered only when it has involved enough devotees to bulk into a perceptible social movement.

Alcoholic intoxication is another way out. Hawaiians took to this haole diversion all too enthusiastically, from the time William Stevenson, formerly of Botany Bay, set up the first still about the beginning of the nineteenth century. Various prohibition laws were passed under missionary influence, only to be repealed again when the traders got the ear of the chiefs, or the chiefs' own bibulous inclinations got the best of them. Walter Murray Gibson, who came to Hawaii as a Mormon missionary, wrote in 1880: "Alas, Hawaiians! look back for only sixty years, since the commencement of your enlightened era, and recall to your mind all your kings and chiefs, that have passed away during these years, and you and all others will be obliged to assent to the statement that many of them died drunkards."

Of the reigning monarch he knew, Kalakaua, Robert Louis Stevenson wrote to a friend in 1889: "His Majesty here . . . is a very fine intelligent fellow, but O, Charles! what a crop for the drink! He carries it too like a mountain with a sparrow on its shoulder. We calculated five bottles of champagne in three hours and a half (afternoon), and the sovereign quite presentable, although perceptibly more dignified at the end." Finally, a report prepared for the Y.M.C.A. during the 1890's sums up: "The liquor consumed in Hawaii in the years 1870–1895 inclusive would fill a trench, five feet wide and four feet deep, reaching from Honolulu Post Office to half a mile beyond Mr. Paul Isenberg's residence at Waialae (6½ miles), and still leave a tank holding 14,000 gallons unused." Of course Hawaiians were by no means the only consumers. Yet from all accounts, in proportion to capacity to pay, they drank their share.

What part withdrawal from haole dominance played in this is impossible to say. In the case of King Kalakaua it may have been a factor. Although he is called "the merry monarch," he suffered, as we shall see, from haole influence. Yet it is questionable whether a king, even in the twilight of the monarchy, can have been seriously threatened with a sense of inferiority.

Haole influence may also have helped drive Liholiho (Kamehameha II) to drink. It was he who first publicly violated the tabus, under pressure from two of his father's widows. It took Dutch courage, the historians say, to bring him to it. But even his father, the great Kamehameha, had become so fond of the product of William Stevenson's still that his haole advisers had to caution him against it. And there is no evidence that Kamehameha I was unable to resist haole dominance; in fact the evidence is all the other way.

Hawaiian commoners suffered heavy losses in property and status as haole prestige grew. Withdrawal from haole inroads more tangible than prestige, perhaps too from haole prestige itself, is a more likely motive for drunkenness among them. Of course, for chiefs and commoners alike, alcohol has a value of its own, the euphoria it brings. Yet as a rule those ruinously addicted to it seem to be trying to get away from something. To sum up, drunkenness has been rather prevalent among Hawaiians, and may have been a refuge from haole dominance in some cases. Yet it has never overwhelmed the Hawaiian people as it apparently has some other peoples under similar but presumably severer stress.

The most conspicuous form of withdrawal from haole prestige has not been adoption of any haole device, but reversion to some part of an ancestral culture other than haole. This appears in many forms. One of them has been stereotyped into what may be called the stage Hawaiian. He lives, or is supposed to live, a happy-go-lucky life; basking on the beach, renouncing the pursuit of worldly goods and all such care-laden haole values. He cherishes other values of his own. Prominent among them are sociable leisure and hospitality. Whatever he has, be it food, women, or children, he shares freely with his associates, and expects the same generosity from them.

These associates include particularly a much wider circle of relatives than haoles keep track of. Not only are sisters, cousins, and aunts counted to the nth degree. The group may even include what old Hawaiian slang calls "calabash relatives," because the kinship consists only in sharing the same bowl of food. Counting such companions as relatives amounts to informal adoption. Indeed, of all forms of Hawaiian sharing, adoption is the most startling to a newcomer. Bringing up children is not necessarily the exclusive prerogative of parents. Grandparents or other relatives may take it over. Many parents, indeed, are perfectly willing to pass their children around. Promising a baby, before its birth, as a gift to a relative or friend, has not been unusual. Correspondingly, orphans or strays are readily welcomed into foster homes.

To some extent this stereotype of Hawaiian life represents the past rather than the present. Yet to this day some Hawaiians exemplify a good deal of it. Is this kind of withdrawal from haole ways really a continuation or revival of a Polynesian pattern? To a considerable extent it is. The high value attached to sociable leisure is thoroughly Polynesian. So is the ready give and take of everything considered worth having, particularly among relatives and quasi-relatives. Even the trappings with which the stereotyped figure is bedecked are Hawaiian, or at least stage Hawaiian. Your carefree type often wears a lei. He goes a-fishing; with throwing net by day, with torch and spear by night. He strums the ukulele. To be sure, his spear nowadays is of haole steel. His torch burns kerosene or even acetylene. Some say the throwing net was introduced by the Chinese. And the ukulele was adapted from a Portuguese importation. Still, all these have been regarded as characteristic of Hawaiians for more than a generation.

This is the same kind of withdrawal as that of another familiar stereotype: the irresponsible, laughing Negro supposed to inhabit the Southern States. Both represent a perfectly real attitude; but both have been exaggerated, somewhat wistfully perhaps, by haoles, who seem to have a hankering for that kind of withdrawal themselves. Indeed, in the late nineteenth century and persisting into the twentieth, a similar attitude was represented by a kind of stage haole: the Beloved Vagabond, the Scholar Gypsy, the Romany Rye. The fact that he bulks larger in literature than in life shows the romantic nature of this withdrawal among haoles. Yet George Borrow did live the life of a gypsy for a while. Thoreau withdrew into a more solitary refuge at Walden. The romantics who got to the South Seas were withdrawing in a similar way. But the fact remains that most of these withdrawals have been temporary.

The stage Hawaiian, usually antedated at least 50 years, and further embellished with a light that never was on sea or land, has been a favorite adornment of tourist advertisements. As this use of the stereotype suggests, playing the carefree Hawaiian has a certain value in the tourist market. It probably helps the lei industry that flourishes about the waterfront when ships come or go, and about beach hotels in the evening. It is a substantial part of the stock in trade of the beach boys, who make a living by taking tourists surf riding, and teaching the more athletic to manage a surfboard themselves. As for the serenaders who stroll about Waikiki in the evening with ukulele and "steel guitar," they stop wherever a blaze of lights or a string of parked cars marks a party, and offer an impromptu concert. In return they expect a freewill offering: a share in the refreshments, some money. In the course of time the practice has become more definitely commercialized. Some of the troupes leave a business card, with name, telephone number, and the reminder "Open for Engagements." So the attitude of the stage Hawaiian in some cases comes down to a costume in which the haole pursuit of money-making can be carried on to advantage. Phonograph records, motion pictures, and radio have widened the market for this commodity. What is going on here, of course, is not withdrawal, but conformity to haole money-making standards, slightly disguised.

In another variant, something of the stage Hawaiian front may mask a deeper withdrawal. Having had their fill of haole condescension, a good many Hawaiians practice a marked reserve toward haoles. They give their confidence only to those who have demonstrated enough sincere friendliness, enough respect for them as human individuals, to deserve it. Some of them even dispense with the gay mask. Their reserve, even then, is usually dignified and courteous, does not pass over, that is, from withdrawal to aggression. One of Beaglehole's informants emphasized this attitude: "An American who has lived for many years in Hawaii but who was not born in the islands said he finds the Hawaiian very hard to meet. . . . He frankly found the Hawaiian displaying great resistance in social relations." Another, born in Hawaii but resident on the American mainland for some years, "characterized the Hawaiians as being extremely sensitive in every way." But the rest of this one's testimony emphasized the happy-go-lucky stereotype.

There is no stereotype of a happy-go-lucky Oriental. That seems not to be an Oriental way of withdrawing. Nor have the Hawaiian born taken it over. Drunkenness, too, is rare, to all appearance, among Oriental immigrants and their Hawaiian-born offspring. Drinking of alcoholic liquor, to be sure, was known to the immigrants before they came. In both China and Japan it is part of the formula for conviviality, as it is among haoles. But both immigrants and their children seem, as a rule, to have restricted it to that role, instead of using it also for a refuge, as individual haoles and Hawaiians do.

Withdrawal by use of another drug, opium, was known to the immigrants from China. In Honolulu during recent years it has not been uncommon for federal officers to seize opium on incoming ships. Naturally they do not find it all. And what slips by them does not all go on to American mainland ports. For every now and then the vice squad of the Honolulu police hears of some opium den, makes a raid, and confiscates opium or its cheaper derivative, *yen shee*. So this way of withdrawal has not gone out of use in Hawaii. Driven under cover as it is, there is no way of measuring its prevalence. Yet, to judge by the energy and progressiveness characteristic of the Chinese part of the community, it cannot be more than the refuge of a few.

Both immigrants and their Americanized children withdraw on occasion into reserve toward haoles. This attitude is inconspicuous. But it may show in the mask provided by their ancestral culture—the expressionless face of the "inscrutable Oriental." (Everybody knows, or should, that Orientals are not "inscrutable" among themselves.) I happen to remember one instance in which the mask was donned suddenly. I took my daughter, then two or three years old, to a Japanese neighborhood to see the woman who, as our "maid," had taken care of her until a short time before. The two were very fond of each other, and the little haole girl ran to the Japanese woman with outstretched arms. A youth on a neighboring lawn smiled at the sight. I smiled at him, sharing his pleasure. But with that his features froze into the traditional mask. He could trust the genuineness of the baby's affection, but not the smile of a grown haole. In that he had reason to suspect condescension. He was withdrawing from haole prestige as manifested in haole complacency.

Reserve toward haoles showed, too, in a standard the young people maintained among themselves. To call one of their number "haolefied" was a condemnation. Now we have seen that as a matter of fact they were all haolefied in every way that matters. Yet they were not entirely haole, could not be if they tried. In other words, they had no chance of being accepted as the kind of person which their community generally regarded as superior. What they did, then, was to take pride in being the kind of person they were by emphasizing the little differences that distinguished them from their ostensible "betters." This standard showed, to take the most conspicuous example, in their speech. Though all were haolefied to the extent that English was the language that "came natural" to them, most of them, to the despair of their schoolteachers, refused to talk the American English held up to them as correct. They held fast to the jargon of Honolulu streets, strongly flavored by Hawaiian, Oriental, and Portuguese influences. The few who did conform to schoolroom standards were condemned as haolefied.

This form of withdrawal, too, has a counterpart among haoles. Members of boys' street-corner gangs in American cities condemn appearance and behavior that is considered well bred. They look and act as tough as they can. Similarly, the books say, in England the cockney scorns to ape the toff. In France I remember hearing an officer of the old nobility marvel at a young fellow who was apparently trying his best to look like a *voyou*. All such people withdraw from the prestige of a class to which they cannot belong by emphasizing whatever sets them apart from it.

Mention of these haole counterparts to forms of withdrawal found in Hawaii may seem irrelevant. There are two reasons for bringing in the comparisons here. First, it may help haoles to get the feel of these bits of behavior practiced by other peoples. Second and more important, it suggests that these forms of withdrawal are not peculiar to Hawaiians or Orientals or any other group alien to ourselves, but are responses to a particular situation which any human being in a similar situation is likely to share.

It is possible that reluctance to appear haolefied, or a related feeling, may have been one factor in the frequent failure of nisei before the war to renounce the Japanese side of their "dual citizenship." Why force themselves on a group which did not welcome them? Still, if this was a factor, it was only one among several. Others were unwillingness to offend the old folks more often than necessary—it was so often necessary; and fear of losing claim to property in Japan. Perhaps most important of all was mere sluggishness, refusal to take these formalities seriously, and shrinking from the embarrassment involved in the process. Honolulu slang summed the matter up in two words: "Waste time!"

Religious Reversion

THE most celebrated form of reversion toward an ancestral culture, under stress from an alien one, is the kind of movement which American anthropologists, with their fondness for clumsy words, have called "nativistic religion." Among a people oppressed and confused by contact with powerful outsiders, a prophet arises. He preaches a new religion—actually, very often, a blend of two old ones, that of local tradition and that introduced by the foreigners. The prophet's listeners are promised that if they accept the faith, and perform its rituals, the old happy days will return. Aggression may be combined with the religious withdrawal in that one of the procedures enjoined on the faithful may be to drive the foreigners out. The fact that spectacular movements of this kind have arisen in America, Africa, and Oceania suggests that they represent a general human response. As for Asia, even a cursory glance at the history of what we think of as the world's great religions hints at the same pattern in the rise of prophets and new sects there. In the United States of our time, various ecstatic cults among Negroes and "poor whites" exemplify the same kind of withdrawal.

Hawaii has never been swept by a mighty outburst of this kind. But there have been plenty of little cults. They were most conspicuous during two periods of unusual stress: first, during the 1830's and 1840's, when Christian missions were near the height of their power, visits from foreign warships were not uncommon, and foreigners were rapidly taking over land and political office; second, during the 1880's, when the native monarchy was tottering to its fall. Lesser movements of the kind have been frequent, perhaps continuous, and were still in evidence during the 1930's.

It is characteristic of the rather mild character of these cults that incitement to open aggression appeared only in the earliest of them; that aggression, even then, was suggested only against the missionaries; and that this attempt at rather drastic reversion was a failure. In 1824, not long after Kapiolani had defied Pele, goddess of volcanoes, a woman who said she was Pele came to the royal town of Lahaina on Maui. She declared herself offended because Kapiolani had eaten the *ohelo* berries that grow about the crater of Kilauea, without first offering her some, as required by old custom. She proclaimed that Kekuaokalani, killed a few years before in the rebellion that followed the abolition of tabus, had sent word from the spirit world that the missionaries must be cast out. To atone for Hawaiian backsliding, a man, a hog, a dog, a white fowl, and a fish must be sacrificed. She threatened to pour her volcanic fires over Lahaina if her demands were not met. Though many believed and trembled, there was no upsurge of religion this time. The most powerful chiefs, emboldened by the abolition of the tabus and by missionary teaching, made fun of the self-styled Pele. At

last she gave up and threw her sacred emblems into a
fire.

In 1830 devotees of two new offshoots of the native
religion were active on the island of Hawaii. One band
worshiped the late king and prophesied his return. The
other credited the hand of a dead child with divine power.

A more typical nativistic cult on the same island a few
years later is reported by the early historians Dibble and
Jarves. Dibble (1843) says:

In Puna, a district at that time under my missionary superin-
tendence, and about thirty miles from my place of residence,
some young men took advantage of the state of things to bring
themselves into notice. They devised a system of religion
half Christian and half heathen. They promulgated that
there were three gods—Jehovah, Jesus Christ, and Hapu
(a young woman who had pretended to be a prophetess and
had lately deceased). They dug up the bones of Hapu,
adorned them with kapas [native cloth], flowers, and birds'
feathers; deposited them in a prominent spot, and marked
about this spot a definite enclosure. This they called *the place
of refuge*. They went from house to house and from village
to village, and exhorted the people with much earnestness
and eloquence, to go to the place of refuge, saying, that the
heavens and earth were about to meet and all who were not
found in the place of refuge would be destroyed.

Jarves concludes as follows: "Multitudes obeyed; a temple
was erected and they continued worshipping day and
night; but the destruction not taking place at the appointed time, hunger compelled many to leave." Dibble
himself later exhorted the people, "mildly exposed the
foolishness and guilt of their conduct," and induced the
repentant to burn the temple of Hapu.

In 1844 Pele came again, but again was not welcomed. *The Polynesian* reported:

A few individuals came . . . to make offering to His Majesty according to the old custom of the land. Upon arriving at the fort, and coming before the Governor, they assumed to be different characters celebrated either in their past history or mythology. One claimed to be Pele; another said he was Kamehameha I. "How is that," said the Governor, "Kamehameha I was a large man and you are a little fellow, you are a liar; guards put him in irons." Their claims to preternatural powers, being submitted to such a scrutiny, they made off with themselves.

In 1845, though, the same journal reported that a prophetess who specialized in healing was having great success:

There now resides at Kawela on the border of Waialua and Koolau of this island [Oahu], an extraordinary young woman, who has excited more attention among the native population than has been elicited by any obscure individual during the present generation. Her name by which she calls herself is Lono [one of the old gods], though her real name is Kalehua. She arrived with her husband a few months since from Hilo, Hawaii, in the character of an inspired doctoress, and has succeeded in winning the belief on the part of the people in every part of the island, that she is capable of performing, and actually accomplishes, the most wonderful cures of any kind of disease. . . . The process of cure is simply (so far as the manual part is concerned) a few aspersions of cold water, and connected with it certain religious rites, such as reading of the Hawaiian scriptures, prayer and confession of sins both secret and public. . . . She professes to be possessed of the spirit of a deceased female who died some 15 years since at the place where she is now residing.

This prophetess declared that she went to heaven every Sunday. She amazed her followers with accounts of the glories she saw there.

In 1846, missionaries answering a questionnaire from Foreign Minister Wyllie reported several such cases. Parker of Kaneohe, Oahu, simply noted in a general way the persistence of belief in persons claiming divine power. His neighbor Emerson of Koolau wrote: "I am told this very day, that a large number (hundreds) are collecting in Koolau to visit a man, who has power to heal diseases miraculously. There have been several such during the year." The report from Johnson of Kauai was similar.

Any emergency might revive remnants of native belief. Chester Lyman wrote in 1847: "No longer ago than last week, when a freshet occurred, threatening to destroy the *kalo* patches and houses, the headman with many of the natives went up with an offering of *kahilis* and *awa* up the stream and supplicated the heathen gods, after the ancient fashion, to put a stop to the waters."

During the middle years of the century outbursts of the kind seem less frequent. Yet in 1866 Mark Twain not only described mourning ceremonies in pagan style for the Princess Victoria, and told tales of vengeance by the Great Shark God, but reported a rumor that the king (Kamehameha V) had advocated a return to the old gods. About 1867 a prophet appeared on the island of Hawaii and proclaimed a new faith. He enjoined common living upon his followers, who wore badges and carried Bibles at their sides. An attempt of the authorities of the Kona district to break up this sect led to one of the rare instances of counteraggression, in which two men were killed. The prophet and some of his most prominent followers were taken to Honolulu, tried, and imprisoned.

In 1881, when a lava flow threatened to destroy the city of Hilo, the Princess Ruth approached Pele in a spirit very different from that of Kapiolani, more than half a century before. This time the princess, going humbly to the edge of the flow, prayed to the goddess, and tossed an offering of haole goods—brandy and red silk, instead of the old awa and red ohelo berries—on the hot lava.

During that same year King Kalakaua, on his return from a world tour, came out for the old gods without reservation. "I have seen the Christian nations, and observed that they are turning away from Jehovah. He represents a waning cause. Shall we Hawaiians take up the worship of a god whom foreigners are discarding? The old gods of Hawaii are good enough for us." (Presumably he spoke in Hawaiian. The English translation is by Reverend Sereno Bishop.)

Instead of promoting a popular religious movement, Kalakaua organized a secret society. Details about it come partly from a report on political conditions in Hawaii prepared for the United States Senate by W. D. Alexander; partly from a pamphlet by James Bicknell, "Hoomanamana—idolatry," undated but plainly contemporary.

The name of the society was *Hale Naua*, sometimes translated Temple of Science, though Naua refers to native rather than haole lore. The date of its founding, in haole chronology, was September 24, 1886; but according to its own constitution it was 40 quadrillions of years after the foundation of the world and 24,750 years after the birth of Lailai, the first woman. Alexander says: "A charter for it was obtained by the King from the Privy Council, not without difficulty, on account of the suspicion that was felt in regard to its character and objects."

To go on with his account:

Its by-laws are a travesty of Masonry, mingled with pagan rites. The Sovereign is styled Iku Hai; the secretary, Iku Lani; the treasurer, Iku Nuu. Besides those were the keeper of the sacred fire, the anointer with oil, the almoner, etc. Every candidate had to provide an "oracle," a *kauwila* wand, a ball of *olona* twine, a dried fish, a taro root, etc. Every member or "mamo" was invested with a yellow *malo* or *pau* (apron) and a feather cape. The furniture of the hall comprised three drums, two *kahilis* or feathered staffs, and two *puloulous* or tabu sticks.

So far as the secret proceedings and objects of the society have transpired it appears to have been intended partly as an agency for the revival of heathenism, partly to pander to vice, and indirectly to serve as a political machine.

Bicknell adds that the Hale Naua had three divisions: *kilo*, devoted to astrology and divination; *kahuna*, devoted to healing, some of it accompanied by incantations, "fetich worship," and Scripture readings; and *kuhikuhipuuone*, devoted to old Hawaiian nature lore, "the scientific phase which holds its meetings in public."

As to equipment and procedure, Bicknell adds:

In the palace is a small room, the only furniture in which is a table with a book lying upon it. The book is David Malo's history of Hawaiian traditions and legends, which after his death came into his daughter's possession; the king obtained it through her husband, John Kapena.

Usually before reading, a circuit of the table is made seven times, after which the book is opened with a show of reverence, and then the credulous owner of the sanctum holds converse, in imagination, with the gods and demi-gods. This book is the basis of the present Hale Naua.

Malo's book, published in 1903 under the title *Hawaiian Antiquities,* is one of the best sources of information on old Hawaiian culture. Malo himself is one of the most distinguished alumni of the old mission school at Lahainaluna, Maui. His interest in the traditions of his ancestors may well have been a case of reversion from haole prestige. Similar work by Kamakau and Kepelino suggests the same response in them. In this connection it is interesting to note that Malo was thought to be involved in the antihaole movement on Maui in 1845, discussed on pages 117–119.

Returning to Kalakaua's secret society, allowance for the hostile bias of the descriptions quoted does not dispel the suggestion that there was as much political hokum in it as religious feeling. It remains a striking attempt at reversion, though of a special kind. Kalakaua also embellished his court with some of the trappings of the ancient nobility—court chanters, hula dancers. But he did not discard the throne, gold-braided uniforms, and other splendors taken over from European courts.

Without attempting to make the list of little cults complete, illustrations of this kind of response may conclude with mention of some of those current among Hawaiians during the 1930's. Beaglehole points out that adherence of Hawaiians to "the less orthodox Christian cults"— the Pentecostal sect, Mormonism, even Roman Catholicism, which is "less orthodox" from the point of view of the dominant element among haoles—involved an attitude somewhat similar to that which has inspired the followers of Hawaiian minor prophets. Mormonism makes an especial appeal to Hawaiians because it gives them status as one of the lost tribes of Israel, and promotes social activities which include hula dancing, in forms that the church approves.

More specifically Hawaiian in membership and appeal were two modern sects, both known loosely among outsiders as "Hawaiian Christian Science." The real name of one of them is Ke Akua Ola, the living God. Beaglehole summarizes its principal tenets:

The founder of this church claims . . . that it emphasizes a cardinal doctrine of Christianity which other sects overlook, namely, the second commandment. The church also believes strongly in the visitation of a father's sins on his son. Hence when misfortune overtakes a person, he must pray to the living God to take away from him the sins of his father. Fasting is particularly valuable for effective action and one seriously troubled by inherited sins is advised to go without food and water for one to three days and spend his time in prayer. There is no division between religious and secular affairs.

If this church reverts at all to ancestral Hawaiian beliefs, there is no suggestion of it here, unless in the absence of a distinction between religious and secular affairs. Indeed, the insistence that it is a purer form of Christianity acknowledges at least partial acceptance of haole prestige. Yet it does involve withdrawal to the extent that it is explicitly by and for Hawaiians.

The other sect, which claims to be the mother church, is called *Ho'omana na'auao o Hawaii*. Reverend Andrew

Bright, then pastor of the church on Cooke Street and High Priest of Kamehameha Lodge (which may be to some extent descended from the Hale Naua), explained its doctrines to me. A full report seems worth while, to bring out his point of view. He repudiated the nickname "Hawaiian Christian Science," and translated the Hawaiian name as "Reasonable Service Church of Hawaii." The phrase ho'omana na'auao occurs in the Hawaiian Bible, Romans 12;7. Bright said the church is a branch of Protestant Christianity, founded in 1853 by his father-in-law, Reverend Andrew Kekipi, who was pastor of the mother church for 40 years. The congregation incorporated in 1911, about the time one faction broke away to form the sect called Ke Akua Ola, discussed above. Another offshoot, still in existence, is called the White Robes or White Garments.

Members of the Reasonable Service church believe that the Hawaiians are descended from ancient Hebrews and Egyptians—a resemblance to Mormonism—and that the old Hawaiian religion came from the same source as Christianity. His church, Bright said, is based on the law of God as revealed in the Ten Commandments, which the members of this faith consider law enough. It was laid down before the Christian missionaries arrived by Kamehameha I, in the *Mamalahoa* (Bright objected to the usual spelling, *Mamalahoe*, translated "Law of the splintered paddle"). He summarized the main provisions of this law as: 1. Love God. 2. Let the great take care of the humble. 3. Let old men, women, and children sleep by the highways in peace.

In most respects the services of this church conform to general Protestant custom. The characteristic which has won it the nickname "Hawaiian Christian Science" is its emphasis on healing. Bright explained its beliefs and practices on this point. The statements in quotation marks were written down immediately after the interview, and are in his own words, or nearly so:

Christian Science says, if you have a sore finger, you think "My finger is not sore," and it is well. We say no. You must find the cause of disease and treat that. It would do no good to cut off the finger. Other fingers might get sore. That would be like trying to get rid of a tree by cutting off the branches. You must cut out the roots. The cause of disease is sin. God says "The wages of sin is death." The patient must find out how he has sinned.

And the cure is repentance. The Catholics say repentance is confessing to a priest and doing as he tells you. That is wrong. The Protestants say repentance is turning about. But a sick man can turn about any number of times without getting well. We say there are three kinds of sin: in thought, in word, and in deed. It is like the three persons of God in the Bible. We repent by praying to God the father, "I have sinned"; to Jesus Christ, the Redeemer, "Forgive me," and to the Holy Ghost, the healer, "Heal me."

In extreme cases, when prayer alone fails, fasting is prescribed. "That is the fourteen-inch gun. First we try the little two-pounders. If they don't work, we try the fourteen-inch gun." In 1901 Reverend John Kekipi treated a woman, a cousin of his, who appealed to him after she had been to a hospital several times, but had refused to submit to the operation advised by a physician. Kekipi told her she must recognize the spiritual as well as the physical disease, and treated her with prayer and fasting. According to Bright's account she sloughed off something like a large intestine, about a fathom long, and knotted. This case got into the newspapers, and for about three years the church had to ride out a storm of opposition from medical men. Bright commented: "If you heal a man without a license, you go to jail. If you kill a man with a license, you're O.K. That is the law of man. It is not the law of God." Reverend Eli Kekipi, son of the founder of the sect and his successor as pastor of the mother church, fasted for 40 days, Bright said; from November 4 to December 14, 1919. He died six days later. At the time of the interview, Bright professed to treat only patients who had been given up by physicians.

Adherents of the Ho'omana na'auao believe that the devil is still alive. Many years ago, while George R. Carter was governor of Hawaii, a woman prominent in Christian Science visited Hawaii on her way to India, where she was going to seek enlightenment. She had several long talks with John Kekipi, and was so impressed that she sent photographs of him to many Christian Science churches, including the mother church in Boston. She was amazed when he told her the devil was still alive, and asked what he is like. Kekipi replied, "He may come on two legs. He may come on four legs. He may come on wings." Bright commented: "Our fathers of the Hawaiian race prayed to wood and stone and bone. Those things became angels." If I understood him rightly, he holds that they are among the forms in which the devil may appear, and that they can be exorcised by prayer. Bones transformed into angels by prayer are pretty clearly the old Hawaiian *unihipili*. Sorcerers, by working magic over bones, were believed to capture the ghost and make it a familiar spirit to run their errands.

I find no record of any new cult springing up in Hawaii among immigrants from China or Japan until news reached Hawaii of the defeat of Japan. At that time some of the immigrants, with whom the superiority of Japan was very like a religion, could not bear to believe that Japan had been defeated. They projected their need of solace in an outburst of rumors to the effect that Japan was victorious, was about to attack Hawaii, and so on. Some took a more definitely religious refuge in adherence to ready-made cults, particularly Seicho-No-Ie (House of Growth), a mixture of Buddhism, Shinto, and Christianity which had been introduced in Hawaii in 1938. Others clustered in new associations with names like Hissho-kai (Association for Absolute Victory) and Shosei-kai (Holy-Righteous Association). A few Buddhist priests, without organizing new sects, became prophets of this escapist movement, though others condemned them. Lind reports: "At the peak of interest in early 1946, these movements clearly assumed the character of a religion and the more rabid proponents manifested the ardor and intolerance of religious zealots."

Among island-born Chinese, reversion to an ancestral religion has been decidedly uncommon. Sau Chun Wong's study of Chinese temples in Honolulu has already been quoted to this effect. This study does report one instance, that of a Hawaiian-born girl who is caretaker of the How Wong Temple on Fort Street. This girl is the daughter of the founder, an immigrant woman who was credited with miracles of healing and prophesy before she came from China. "The present caretaker is unmistakably proud of her mother who, she claims, prayed with such concentration that even the entrance of bandits did not break her trance." As an instance of exceptional influence of an immigrant parent who was herself decidedly exceptional, this seems to represent continuance of old-country belief rather than reversion to it as a refuge from haole dominance.

Reversion into ancestral religion, in a much calmer spirit, has already been suggested as one of several factors in the continued interest of many nisei in Buddhism. The same tendency, and in a similar mild form, may have helped the spread of two sects which arose in Japan during the nineteenth century. Both were founded by Japanese women of humble status. To consider how far they conformed, in Japan, to the "nativistic" would be too long an excursion from our subject. One of the sects called Konko-kyo emphasizes worship of the Golden Light deity. The other, and far the more influential in Hawaii, is Tenrikyo, founded in 1837 on the basis of revelations announced by the housewife Miki Nakayama. Its first church in Honolulu was opened in 1929. In 1933 it had six churches in Hawaii, three of them in Honolulu. In 1936 one of its adherents told me it had 15 churches in Honolulu alone.

Description of a typical service at the church in the McCully district will show some of the characteristics of Tenrikyo. The congregation was seated in Japanese fashion on cushions laid on the mat floor. Shoes and sandals had been left on the steps. Those who took a prominent part, men as well as women, wore formal black kimonos. One priest's kimono was decorated with white embroidery. The first part of the service consisted of chanting hymns to simple tunes of narrow compass. The singing of some of them was accompanied by formal mo-

tions of the hands. Between hymns the congregation
bowed to the three shrines, typically Shintoist in their
plain white wood, round mirrors, zigzag strips of white
paper, and offerings of vegetables. After bowing, all
clapped hands four times, then repeated the bowing and
clapping. During the singing of the last hymn several
women, accompanied by a small orchestra of ancient Japanese instruments, danced on the raised floor before the
shrines. Their formal motions suggested a simplified theatrical dance.

Then a table was set up before the congregation, spread
with a purple cloth and set with a tray holding a teapot
and glasses. A woman told how the faith had cured her
of asthma. The priestess gave what seemed to be a sermon. Finally food trays were laid on the matting, and
the people gathered about them to chat and partake of
sake, sweetened and colored water, rice cakes, pickled
vegetables, and raw fish with soy and mustard sauce.

Though the bows and dances were performed solemnly,
the tone of the gathering was lighthearted. During the
service some little girls played a Japanese game at the
top of the steps, separated only by a wooden screen from
the auditorium. While most of the congregation was
gathered about the food trays, several patients took turns
sitting before the priestess, who prayed with them. As
an interested spectator, I was invited to share in the
luncheon, and several devotees told me how they or their
relatives had been cured of various ills.

Interest in this sect among the Hawaiian born probably
involves reversion. Costume, symbols, and procedure are
not only Japanese, but have an antique air. The emphasis
on public testimony about cures, on the other hand, sug-

gests influence from Christian Science. Testing the accuracy of that suggestion would be, again, outside our province. It would be very pertinent to know the strength of reversion from haole prestige, as compared with that of relief from other anxieties, such as that due to illness. But there seems to be no way to find out, unless by analysis of individual cases too searching to be undertaken here.

All the cultures represented in Hawaii had a share in a short-lived but dramatic healing cult that reached its height on the island of Oahu in 1927. It seems to have had no prophet, and the beliefs involved in it were never formulated. Presumably they varied widely among different devotees. Clearly, though, they involved curious transformations of old lore.

The proper birthplace for chiefs of the highest rank on Oahu in ancient times was Kukaniloko on the upland plains of Helemanu, near the present town of Wahiawa.* A cluster of boulders there was credited with magical powers. During the labors of childbirth chiefly mothers lay on one of the boulders, which was supposed to relieve pain and sanctify the rank of the child. Tradition traced the repute of the stones back to the birth there of Kapawa, grandson of a chief from Kahiki (Tahiti; later, foreign parts in general). According to the usual reckoning of genealogies, the time of that event would be about the beginning of the twelfth century A.D. Of the birth there of Kakuhihewa, who became a famous king of Oahu, Fornander relates: "Forty-eight chiefs of the high-

---

* Kukaniloko, birthplace of chiefs. *Hawaiian Almanac and Annual,* 1920.

est rank . . . were present at the ceremony of cutting the navel string of the new-born chief, and the two sacred drums named Opuku and Hawea announced the important event to the multitude." So great was the fame of Kukaniloko that even Kamehameha, first king of all the islands, though he came from the island of Hawaii, wished to have his son born at this sanctuary.

About 1925 the society called Daughters of Hawaii took charge of the site to preserve it as a historic monument.* There were a number of boulders about, most of them embedded in the ground. A large upright one was said to have been brought from near-by Kaukonahua gulch about 1882 by George Galbraith, then owner of the surrounding land, and set up as a marker. This is on the authority of "an old native." Now this seems just the kind of story with which a Hawaiian would be apt to mislead outsiders prying into sacred mysteries. Why should Galbraith have gone to all that trouble, when there were plenty of boulders already on the spot? However that may be, the Daughters of Hawaii credited the story and had this particular boulder removed to another site not far away, with the idea of restoring Kukaniloko more nearly to its ancient condition.

This activity seems to have revived interest in the stones—particularly the big one that had been moved, and a smaller one that stood beside it in its new position. First to use it as a touchstone at this time are said to have been Filipinos in quest of luck at gambling. Then word got around that it had healing power, appealing to the anxiety about disease that has been prominent in so many of the little cults of Hawaii.

* Wahiawa's healing stone. *Ibid.*, 1928.

Pilgrims began to visit the stone, many of them with various infirmities. Stories of marvelous cures spread about. The devotees increased in numbers until, during 1927, throngs visited the stones every week end.

Heirs to different cultures made their appeals for help in the various ways learned from their ancestors. Hawaiians decked the stones with flower leis, Filipinos and Portuguese with rosaries. Chinese, Japanese, and Koreans burned incense sticks before them. Haoles, for some reason, set them in a concrete base and put a wire fence around them. Perhaps they feared the development of a retail trade in pieces chipped from the stones.

Some did profit from the situation in a business way. Dealers in food, leis, and incense sticks got concessions from the government and set up booths near by. The manager of the Wahiawa Water Company had a box placed for the numerous offerings of money, and deposited them in the bank as a community welfare fund. Unbelievers living in the neighborhood, disturbed by the throngs, asked to have the stones removed as a menace to health; but the board of health, after due bacteria counts, decided there was no emergency.

A whole cycle of myths sprang up about the stones. Hawaiian devotees declared that a pilgrim, after gazing steadily at the large one, might be rewarded with a vision of a woman and child (Mary and the infant Jesus?). Then, if he leaped the fence and hung a lei over the stone, he could depart with his prayer granted. It was said that a Filipino stole the first money box, containing about $300, and was punished by prompt and mysterious death; and that another met the same fate for disrespectfully pushing the stone while it was being moved. This is quite

like tales told in the old days of punishment for violation of a tabu.

The craze died out almost as quickly as it had arisen.
On October 10, 1931, the Honolulu *Star-Bulletin* pub-
lished a reminiscent article under the heading "The Once
Hawaiian Sacred Stone Mecca Is Now Silent Place."

What had all this to do with withdrawal from haole
dominance? The question is not easy to answer. The
anxiety obviously assuaged by visits to the stones was
that over sickness, though appeals were apparently made
for help in other ways, too. But it is noticeable that the
devotees included all the kinds of people in Hawaii except haoles, if we retain the definition of haole common
in the islands, which does not include Portuguese. Many
haoles came out of curiosity, and it is possible that a few
may have been carried along by the high tide of faith; but
it still remains generally true that haoles did not partici-
pate. Add to this the similarity of this movement to others
of "nativistic" type in Hawaii, and for that matter all
over the world, and the suggestion is strong that pressure of haole dominance was one of the motives, however transmuted, behind this little outburst of faith.

During the 1930's a cult of the general type under discussion was prevalent among Filipinos in Hawaii. Filipinos had been excluded from this study in the attempt
to bring it within manageable scope. One reason for leaving them out, in spite of their large numbers, was that
there were at that time so few Hawaiian-born Filipinos,
and those few so young, that Filipinos did not afford evidence of change between immigrant and island-born generations comparable to that available for Chinese and Jap-

anese. Another was that the Filipinos had been long and heavily influenced by haole culture—first from the Spanish, later from the Americans—before they reached Hawaii. So change in Hawaii among them was somewhat obscured by earlier change.

For these reasons no attempt was made to study the new cult among Filipinos. Yet from the point of view now under discussion, its very existence is significant. The Filipinos, as the latest comers to Hawaii, had the lowest status among the peoples there. Most of them were still plantation laborers. Attempts to make headway in other occupations were only beginning. So they were subject to more stress at that time than others. The appearance of a new cult among them was to be expected. Only a few bizarre, superficial characteristics of the cult were observed. The devotees went barefoot, and let their hair and beards grow long. One of their forms of worship was to hold meetings at night in cemeteries. The police took the view that such conduct was unlawful and occasionally raided those gatherings.

Recreative Reversion

A MILD type of reversion was prevalent during the 1930's among people of both Hawaiian and Oriental descent. Its development was noted in *Social Process in Hawaii* for 1937 by Romanzo Adams, who at that time had been teaching sociology at the University of Hawaii for 17 years:

It is easy for one who has been in contact with Hawaii's young people for a long time to note the beginning of a change in attitude toward the culture of their ancestors.

Fifteen or twenty years ago one was impressed by the tendency on the part of Hawaiian born and educated young people to depreciate the customs and ideas of their parents. As American citizens they were trying to win an economic status superior to what their parents possessed and they felt that the persistence of old country traditions was burdensome and that it was an obstacle to achievement.

But in the more recent years young people of the same age—the younger brothers and sisters or, perhaps, the nephews and nieces—are undergoing a change of attitude. Viewing the situation from the standpoint of a more advanced stage in economic adjustment and acculturation they evaluate old country customs more discriminatingly. They find some things that seem to be permanently good and there is beginning to be a tendency to idealize the traditional ways followed by their ancestors.

Professor Adams was writing, of course, about young people of other than haole descent. Those whom he knew best—and perhaps no one knew them better—were university students, the more intellectually sophisticated of their generation. In other words, they were just the ones who would have been least likely to seek help from such a source as the sacred stones of Wahiawa. It was among these—not necessarily university trained, but at least of a wider range of interests than average—that the "tendency to idealize traditional ways" was most in evidence.

Hawaiians, in the more public manifestations of interest in their old culture, emphasized the picturesque. This has already been suggested in the sketch of the "stage Hawaiian." Large numbers took part in occasional displays, such as the annual parades on June 11, Kamehameha Day. Men of the Order of Kamehameha wore over their haole clothes paper replicas of the red and yellow feather cloaks of high chiefs. (Real feather cloaks, now rare museum pieces, were never numerous enough to constitute a uniform; not even a court uniform.) Floats covered with greenery bore troupes of hula dancers. Women on horseback, with long, richly colored skirts trailing behind on both sides, portrayed the *pa'u* riders who were a dashing spectacle in the days of the monarchy. (Pa'u meant originally the native wrapped skirt or kilt, mostly of bark cloth. Voluminous ones of haole fabrics were a special riding costume. Even in the palmy days of the side saddle, Hawaiian women rode astride.)

Only one shade less public was an occasional "Holoku Ball." The *holoku* or Mother Hubbard dress was introduced by missionary women as soon as they arrived. Mrs. Thurston wrote of the very first sewing circle, organized at Kailua, Hawaii, iin 1820 before the pioneer company reached Honolulu: "The four women of distinction were furnished with calico patchwork to sew—a new employment for them. The dress was made in the fashion of 1819. The length of the skirt accorded with Brigham Young's rule to his Mormon damsels—*have it come down to the tops of the shoes.*" While haole fashions changed through the years, the holoku remained so nearly the same that by 1865 it looked strange to Mrs. Mary Anderson, newly arrived from America: "The women's dresses are made just like yoke night-gowns, falling to the feet without being confined at the waist at all." It became a characteristic Hawaiian costume. Conservative elderly Hawaiian women wear them still. At the "Holoku Ball" variants of this humble garment in the most gorgeous colors and fabrics, with exaggerated trains that could be held up while dancing by a loop around the wrist, became a badge of pride in being Hawaiian.

Glimpses of Polynesian Hawaii, some of them carefully authentic, were furnished by pageants, which during the 1930's became so linked with the thought of Hawaiian tradition that some haoles considered the pageant itself a characteristic of native culture. Actually, of course, though the subject matter was Polynesian, this way of presenting it was haole. Moreover, most of these spectacles have been promoted by haoles. The first of which I find record (in the *Hawaiian Almanac and Annual*) was in 1913, in connection with a floral parade. It represented the landing of Kamehameha I on Oahu. A notable pageant formed part of the Mission Centennial celebration in 1920. An account of another, in the *Annual* for 1926, self-consciously emphasizes the haole point of view: "A pageant of so-called old-time incantations to Pele, to return her volcanic fires, was given with much imaginary ancient ceremony and sacred pomp at Kilauea, at dusk of Saturday, March 24th, for which much preparation had been made by certain Hiloites promoting and directing its representation, 'not as incantations of old-time worship of Pele,' said its manager, 'but a commercializing of ancient paganism.'" A series of pageants, probably the high mark of Hawaiian pageantry, was performed during the Cook Sesquicentennial in 1928.

Although haole initiative predominated in all of these, a good many Hawaiians were willing collaborators. During the 1930's two "Hawaiian villages" not far from the tourist hotels at Waikiki were manned and at least partly planned by Hawaiians. The Lalani village, an enterprise of the part-Hawaiian Mossman family, fairly often staged pageants, naturally on a smaller scale than those mentioned. A "Hawaiian Thanksgiving" there in 1935, though it included turkey cooked in the *imu* (earth oven), also portrayed a *ho'okupu,* or ceremonial gift exchange, following Hawaiian custom as nearly as it could be recalled.

As reversion on the part of Hawaiians to their ancestral culture all this is plainly fragmentary and superficial. One value involved in it is show, acting here to preserve bits of the old culture rather than accelerate choice of the new. The interest in display also suggests that, far from involving any denial of haole prestige, these spectacles are in part defensive, an attempt to lift the Hawaiian heritage to a higher place in the esteem of haoles. It has been so far successful that appreciation by haoles of these displays pretty surely gives some relief from haole prestige. This is relief by way of disguised conformity, an element found also in the more commercialized versions of the "stage Hawaiian" role. But the element of disguised desperation, characteristic of more sincere and thorough cases of the "happy-go-lucky Hawaiian," is not evident in this parading type of reversion. Withdrawal here acts in a different way. On the face of it, display is the opposite of withdrawal; and indeed, withdrawal here is not only disguised but subordinate to the other elements just mentioned. Still, insofar as relief from haole prestige is obtained through pride in the ancestral tradition, there is at least a temporary withdrawal from submergence in haole concerns.

The unusual reversion of David Kaapu had points of similarity with both these types, but went farther than either, except that there was nothing desperate about it. During the 1930's Kaapu gave a continuous performance that might be called a one-man pageant. He built himself a thatched house, as nearly old Hawaiian as he could manage, at Punaluu on the windward side of Oahu. For clothing he wore only a malo or loincloth, at least during the heat of the day. He raised taro under water in the old way, pounded it into poi, caught fish by traditional methods, and so fed himself as Hawaiians used to do. To be sure, display and even commercialism were present in this spectacular reversion. David's place was not far from the highway on which tourists were driven around the island. He became, for a small admission fee, one of the sights. Sometimes he regaled a party with a Hawaiian feast, thus adding more substantially to his income. Still, he might very well have been able to make more money in other ways. He gave visitors the impression of genuine interest in his Polynesian heritage, and pride in exemplifying a way of life in which almost anyone could find something to admire.

Of course the reversion of David Kaapu was far from complete. He did not return to anything in Hawaiian culture which haoles find objectionable. No offerings before images of the old gods. No departure from monogamy. (As it happened, his wife was a haole.) His mother and sister lived in a haole house near his Hawaiian one. Even if he had tried his best, he could not have returned completely to old Hawaiian ways of living and thinking.

More frequent has been supplementing a mainly haole life with an interest in Hawaiian tradition, which commonly specialized in some particular activity. Charles W.

Kenn, while employed by the Honolulu playground commission, promoted displays of old Hawaiian sports, some of which had been all but forgotten. His interest in Polynesian Hawaii was particularly broad. He organized an informal society which met to hear papers on Hawaiian culture. His magazine article, "I Am a Hawaiian" (*Paradise of the Pacific*, 1936), is a profession of faith.

A similar interest, even more scholarly, was shown by Mrs. Elizabeth Heen, who in 1936 wrote a master's thesis at the University of Hawaii on "The Hawaiians of Papakolea." This was in part a study of this settlement as an example of problems involved in the present social situation of Hawaiians; partly also a study of remnants of Hawaiian tradition surviving in this most Hawaiian part of modern Honolulu.

In the case of Mrs. Kawena Pukui this kind of interest has developed into a lifetime occupation. Mrs. Pukui spends her days translating old Hawaiian texts in the Bishop Museum, and has collaborated with haole ethnologists in a number of publications. All of these people —Kenn, Mrs. Heen, Mrs. Pukui—are by descent part-Hawaiian. They have chosen to emphasize the Hawaiian part, but in most of their daily routine are content to follow the dominant haole pattern.

The hula dance has been the point of focus for a good deal of recent interest among Hawaiians in their old culture. Its picturesque display value is clearly one reason. Another, pretty surely, has been change in attitude toward the hula among haoles. The old standard—condemnation by the righteous, enjoyment by the worldly, of what both took for a lascivious spectacle—has gradually yielded to appreciation of an admirable art form, in which the erotic element came to be played down rather than up.

An outstanding example of this change, and a leader in it, was Nathaniel Emerson, member of one of the prominent missionary families. In 1892, in an article which was largely a defense of missionaries against the charge of suppressing native sports, he wrote: "How little power of control . . . the missionary had, may be judged from the fact that in spite of his declared opposition to the hula, that relic of heathenism still survives and from time to time the altars of the obscene Laka * send forth their baleful light, as the waning fires are fed by high patronage at home, or are replenished by the offerings of pilgrims from abroad." Later on, the interest in Hawaiian culture shown by this article broadened to include an admiration of the hula, which inspired Emerson to make a thorough study of it. His book, *Unwritten Literature of Hawaii*, published by the Smithsonian Bureau in 1909, centers about the hula and is still the most detailed publication on the subject.

The revival of the hula under the patronage of Kalakaua represented not only reversion to native culture but also aggression against the missionaries. As time went on, the element of reversion remained, but that of aggression faded out with haole disapproval. For some years, early in the twentieth century, interest in ancient versions of the hula was fostered particularly by Mrs. Emma Fern, a descendant of chiefs. She visited old hula teachers on different islands, and became celebrated as a teacher herself.

* Patron goddess of the hula.

Her pupils used to perform in a once famous "hula house" in the Kapahulu district of Honolulu. Though still somewhat suspect among the righteous, these performances were no commercialization of sex appeal but—I have it on the high authority of Mrs. Lahilahi Webb of Bishop Museum—faithful performances of old dances, some of which had been nearly forgotten.

An example of scholarly interest in the hula during recent years was a demonstration of old hulas from the island of Kauai, given by Keahi Luahine at the Honolulu Academy of Arts (which was endowed by a missionary family) in 1936. Quotation from the program will show how much of the old tradition is still preserved by a few:

In old Kauai the general scheme or pattern of a group of ancient hula dances was carefully planned. One part of the program led to another, whether the dances were of the same type or not, and the whole had its *kaona*, or special inner meaning.

The story of tonight's program is as follows:

The first two dances, the *hula Pele*, followed by the *hula hoe*, or canoe paddling hula, signify "The goddess Pele coming on a canoe.

The *hula ki'i*, or dance of the wooden images, conveys the idea that the spirits represented by the images shall man Pele's canoe. The dog deity, *Ku-ilio-loa*, welcomes Pele ashore and so the dog dance or *hula ilio* follows. Then comes a feast in which a hog is served, hence the hog dance or *hula pua'a*.

But the hog must be cooked and the house built to receive the royal guest and so there is the *hula ka-la'au* or stick dance (*la'au* meaning stick or wood).

After the feast comes the entertainment, a royal one befitting the Goddess Pele, and the *pahu* (large drum) is brought forth for the *hula pahu*. The guest is a beloved one and so she is welcomed with the dance of all favorite children, the *hula kuhi*, a simple sitting and gesturing hula.

This *kaona* or inner meaning was very important in ancient Hawaii and is remembered today among the older people of the Islands.

Attempts to revive Hawaiian crafts, such as plaiting in *lauhala* (pandanus leaf) and making bark cloth (tapa) involve a similar light reversion. They have had but slight success. The market for lauhala articles has kept that industry alive, but tapa making has not been resurrected. Virtually all the tapa sold in Hawaii of late years, and some of the pandanus articles too, have been imported from Samoa.

Reversion of this type is prominent also among the island born of Oriental stock; even the Chinese, with whom acculturation seems to have progressed so far that very little stress remains. It resembles what has just been noted among Hawaiians in that it is strongest among the intellectuals; it emphasizes recreative and esthetic aspects of the old cultures; and it seems to respond to the value of picturesque display.

Interest in Chinese drama, or American adaptations of it, is an outstanding illustration. Fondness for the theater was pronounced even in the rural village of the Canton delta, and was brought to Hawaii by the immigrant generation. The first reference I find—and it claims to be an innovation—is the following advertisement in the *Pacific Commercial Advertiser* of September 6, 1879, when Chinese immigration had not quite reached its peak:

Special Notice.
The undersigned, managers of
—the—
CHINESE THEATRE!
would respectfully bring to the notice
of the public that their
PLACE OF AMUSEMENT
—WILL BE—
Opened on or about the 11th inst.,
—by a—
FIRST CLASS COMPANY
—of over—
Eighty performers!

———

Plays representative of Chinese Life and
Manners will be presented, with all the
necessary dresses and stage setting, and
in a manner that has
Never Before Been Attempted!
No expense will be spared to contribute
to the comfort of our patrons, and a
visit to our Performances will satisfy
the most fastidious.
Respectfully,
Tung Hing Tong & Co.

Since few Chinese at that time could read English, the
appeal to haole interest is already evident. Yet the backlog
of support for such an enterprise had to be Chinese. This
theater flourished for some time, until its strident orchestra brought complaints from the neighbors. Its successor
was built in what was then a more out-of-the-way site,
King Street by Nuuanu stream. In September, 1894, this
was condemned and torn down. The *Pacific Commercial*

Advertiser, in announcing the sale of the building at auction, said there was no immediate prospect of another. But the same newspaper, in 1901, described a Chinese theater already in operation at that time. This may be the building in "Tin Can Alley" still pointed out in the 1930's as the "old Chinese theater," though used then mostly for Japanese motion pictures. Charles Taylor noted that in 1906 "The city maintains two theaters, both under the management of the Chinese. One is called the 'Old,' the other the 'New' theater." He said enough of the performance and audience to show that the plays were Chinese.

After annexation to the United States, the immigration authorities admitted occasional troupes of Chinese actors under bond, on condition of their returning to China. In 1920 a company of women arrived, and they and their successors used the Oahu theater on Maunakea Street continuously for about 10 years. Appearance of women on the stage is itself a departure from old Chinese practice, whereby female as well as male parts were taken by men. But this innovation developed in China. Otherwise these itinerant companies have followed Chinese dramatic style in general: emphasizing conventional symbolism in gesture and make-up; minimizing scenery and properties except for gorgeous costumes, also conventionalized to represent standard characters; and giving long programs of traditional pieces, in which some of the lines were spoken, others sung, while the action was emphasized throughout by music—itself stiff with symbolic conventions—from an orchestra seated on the stage.

Theater going among immigrant Chinese of course represents continuation of the old culture rather than reversion to it. But the island-born generations seem not to have carried their general departure from old-country ways into this field. With them, American as they are, this is reversion, as the term is used here.

In Honolulu during the 1930's there were two Chinese dramatic organizations. The older of them, Gut Hing Kung So, had been organized by immigrant actors, but by 1930 its membership included many of the island born. The continuity from generation to generation typical of this activity is shown by the prominence of the Ma family in the association. In 1936 Ma Wah was president, and the leading part in the annual play was taken by Miss Ma Mei Yong. She is an island-born girl who had spent several years in China as the protégée and pupil of an actress, also of the Ma clan, who had visited Honolulu as a member of the women's troupe just mentioned. At a banquet some weeks after the performance, Ma Tai Soo awarded a gold medal to Ma Mei Yong in recognition of her achievements as an actress.

More frequent public appearances were made by the Tan Sing Dramatic Club, an organization recruited largely among island-born Chinese. The club arose in 1930 from the ashes of a similar organization three years older. In January, 1936, it was awarded 1,000 yuan ($295) by the overseas commission of the Chinese Government. The Tan Sing club had a building on Kukui Street near Nuuanu, with a gate in ornamental latticework surmounted by a sign in English. Though most of the repertoire was traditional, this club also performed modern adaptations, some of which even involved the use of scenery, and supplied coaches, musicians, and actors for plays by other organizations.

Adaptations and imitations in English represent a dilution of Chinese culture, comparatively easy for haolefied youth to enjoy. A number of these have been composed in Honolulu. About 1925 Chang Hoon wrote a play in Chinese, which was translated into English by M. Sing Au and published under the title *The Broken Chain*. In 1934 a play by Mrs. Peter Y. Chang was performed by a women's club of the University of Hawaii at a performance in the Honolulu Academy of Arts. Plays given at New Year performances in 1935 were written by Jennie Fong and Peace Tan. The American-made *Yellow Jacket* was given twice during the 1930's by student casts. Another adaptation, "Lady Precious Stream," was performed in 1935 and 1936.

Chinese puppet shows, though rarer, were given twice in 1936: once at the New Year program of the Academy of Arts, and again at the Chung Shan school festival.

For some years Honolulu had no exclusively Chinese theater. Chinese motion pictures were shown occasionally; for example, at the Park Theater in 1936, the comedy "Two Countrymen," with dialogue in Cantonese. Construction of the Golden Wall Theater on School Street began in 1937. The theater opened during the 1938 New Year season, with nightly plays by a troupe from Canton. The performances showed in several respects the influence of European plays and motion pictures, but retained Chinese conventions such as a tufted staff to symbolize a horse, a gesture to open a nonexistent door, and the nonchalant property man, who shuffled about the stage in shirtsleeves, on such errands as tucking a pillow under the head of a fallen hero.

Dancing was a conspicuous gap in the immigrant

Chinese culture. Here the island born added a recent importation. Gladys Li of Honolulu, daughter of Dr. and Mrs. K. F. Li, studied for two years with Chu Kuei Fang of Peking, a leader in adaptation for separate performance of dances based on the classical drama. On her return she appeared at receptions at the governor's residence and Chinese consulate and in special programs at the Royal Hawaiian Hotel. She arranged and coached the first Moon Festival programs at the Honolulu Academy of Arts. Largely through her influence, a number of the island born developed an interest in Chinese dancing.

Other bits of reversion among the island born mount up to rather an impressive total. Revival of interest in Chinese athletics was shown by the organization in 1936 of a Chinese Physical Culture Association. The members met in the club rooms at 34 Kapena Lane to practice Chinese boxing, and fencing with ancient weapons like broadswords, halberds, trident spears, and long staves. The association gave occasional public exhibitions. (One motive behind this revival may have been a flare-up of Chinese national spirit in resentment of Japanese aggression.)

Someone on the faculty of Mid-Pacific Institute, most of whose students were of Oriental descent, organized in 1911 a Kite Day which became an annual event. Kites representing dragons, lanterns, butterflies, warriors, and other fantastic forms were flown in competition for prizes. They made such a spectacular display that it attracted throngs of tourists. In 1930 the event was dropped because, as the Institute's quarterly bulletin explained, "the students themselves felt they did not know enough about making the really interesting and beautiful speci-

mens such as were made in bygone days." Alumni formed
a kite school to revive the contest in 1935, and the idea of
an annual kite day was taken over by the municipal recreation commission.

Chang Hoon, already mentioned as a playwright, carried esthetic reversion farther than anyone else en-
countered in this inquiry. Though a fairly young man,
he seemed more at home with the language of his ancestors than with English, and his genuine impulse to
artistic creation expressed itself in Chinese forms. He
seemed deeply absorbed in this pursuit. Besides the play
translated as *The Broken Chain,* he had when I knew him
composed words and music of six Chinese songs. Haole
influence showed in the fact that he had, with American
assistance, harmonized the melodies. One of his difficulties in arranging for publication of the songs was
to get the words translated into English without losing
their flavor. He illustrated this for me by giving, in hesi-
tant English, an abstract of one of the texts:

The poet is awakened by soft, sweet music. He follows
the sound into the garden, where he sees what at first appears to be a glowing cloud. As he comes nearer, the cloud
takes form as a beautiful girl.

After this explanation he sang the song as translated
for him by one of his more thoroughly Americanized
students of Chinese music. The words were full of stereotyped phrases from Tin Pan Alley. Chang Hoon said
sadly: "My song was classical. This is more like jazz."

In 1936 a former pupil and distant relative of his, Miss
Rose Chang, published an adaptation from a Chinese folk
song, translated as "China Flower." An American band-

master, Leonard Hawk, had helped her arrange and harmonize it.

A number of island-born girls took enough interest in Chinese music to become skillful players of the "butterfly harp" and "moon guitar," and singers to its accompaniment. Not infrequently they appeared before audiences made up largely of haoles, particularly at the Honolulu Academy of Arts.

Some of the Chinese holidays attract interest of this kind. Those of which the young people are particularly fond are Chinese New Year; the Ching Ming festival or Decoration Day; and the harvest moon festival or Chinese Thanksgiving. Other values that have helped perpetuate these celebrations have already been discussed. The one that fits particularly into the pattern of recreative reversion is that of picturesque display.

When the more prosperous young people of Chinese descent build homes for themselves, the fundamental construction and the mechanical appurtenances are thoroughly haole. But rather recently—about 1930—Chinese decorative touches began to appear even about the exterior: eaves upturned at the corners, staggered latticework, windows of round or other ornamental form. This was particularly noticeable in the Bingham tract lying seaward of the University of Hawaii campus. Because of the predominance here of new, part-modernistic and part-Chinese houses, this district was known in Honolulu slang of the 1930's as "Chinese Hollywood." A few public buildings have borrowed even more of Chinese exterior design. Perhaps the first was the Chinese Christian Church. Though designed by a haole architect, Hart

Wood, this apparently expressed pride of the congregation in their Chinese heritage. Similar decoration had advertising value in two buildings opened in 1938: the Golden Wall Theater and a new building for the Wo Fat Restaurant.

Inside the homes, Chinese decoration is much more in evidence. One of Professor Keesing's students summarized this: "In nearly every Chinese home in Hawaii, there are some works of art, as embroidered scrolls, framed embroidered omens, teak or camphorwood furnishings, cushions, tapestries, porcelains, Canton dishes, etc. Chinese American school teachers especially have a mania for rugs and porcelains." Selecting school teachers for mention is not accidental but corroborates the suggestion already made, that this kind of reversion is especially evident among the more intellectual.

Recreative reversion toward Japanese culture has followed the same general course as toward Chinese and Hawaiian. Minor differences, some of which go back to the ancestral culture while others may reflect different circumstances in Hawaii, will appear in the following review.

Nisei interest in Japanese drama can be illustrated by three performances given in Honolulu during 1936. Most Japanese of the three, though based on a Buddhist legend from India, was *Prince Ajatasatru*, given by a nisei cast at a banquet in honor of 40 of the oldest immigrant Japanese. This was said to be the first of its type to be seen in Hawaii. The other two productions were both of the same play, an English adaptation called *The Darkness of the Dawn*. One was by the Theater Guild of the University of Hawaii, the other by young people of the Soto Buddhist mission.

All three were coached or at least counseled by Zenjiro Hosokawa, whose stage name is Shusui Hisamatsu. Trained in Japan, he had settled in Honolulu in 1918. His wife was Hawaiian born, and both she and their daughters became adept in his art. In 1920 he had organized the Shinsei Gekidon or New Voice theatrical troupe, which played not only in Hawaii but also along the American Pacific Coast from Canada to Mexico. This one man, not himself Hawaiian born, was the leading influence in the continuance of Japanese drama in the islands at that time. But at least he found a ready response among the nisei.

A related interest was noted by Paul Tajima in a study of Japanese language schools: "Japanese classic dancing is very popular among the younger generation who wear colorful kimonos and go to the large dancing parties by hundreds and thousands. A recent notable thing is that the schools which devote more attention to these subjects are drawing more students." This style of dancing, which emphasizes the pictorial effect of posture and costume rather than rhythmic movement, is adapted from the stylized pantomime of old Japanese plays.

Dances of theatrical type appealed particularly to girls, but interest in Japanese dancing included also a distinctly masculine variety, the sword dance (*kembu*). This involves strokes, feints, and parries from old military swordsmanship, executed in formal style to the accompaniment of a chant. Most of the chants, too, are definitely military in spirit, but not necessarily nationalistic. For instance, one of those used in Honolulu extolled the manly virtue that shone in the eyes of Napoleon and George Washington. Some, indeed, are not military at all, but meditations on natural beauty. In these, as a rule, the sword remains sheathed throughout, and the gesturing is done with a fan.

As in the case of Japanese drama, enthusiasm for this style depended largely on one leader. But this one was himself Hawaiian born. During the day, as Junsui Nagao, he worked at a garage in downtown Honolulu. But most of his evenings were spent in the role of Shuko, an honorific name conferred on him by the organization of sworddancing experts in Japan. (He had learned, though, in Hawaii, from teachers of the immigrant generation.) He was instructor to four classes in different parts of Honolulu, and occasionally gave radio performances of the chants that go with sword dances. He represents esthetic reversion developed beyond a diverting hobby into an avocation.

Descendants of Okinawans had especial need of pride in their heritage, for they suffered not only from haole domination, but from a traditional inclination of other Japanese to look down on them. Of all their old culture, the dances seem especially rich in the distinctive quality that meets this need. In contrast to the restrained dignity of most Japanese dancing, Okinawan dances are lively, and the costumes are gay to the verge of gaudiness. For example, for one spirited solo performance, the male dancer wears a fantastic headdress, a short jacket colored pea green and magenta, and black trousers bound below the knee with crossed white strips, a little like puttees. Another dance, performed by a man and a woman, is a pantomime of courtship. Advances, coy retreats, and circlings culminate in an exchange of scarves, and final steps with hands joined.

Skill in these dances was imparted to the Hawaiian born by several teachers. In 1936 a public performance was given during the silver jubilee of the magazine *Jitsugyo-no-Hawaii*. Another in 1938 accompanied dedication of a new Buddhist temple in the Kalihi district. A little later a third was given, for all Honolulu, at the Academy of Arts. (An outside influence in arranging the last was the writer, a haole eager to share his delight in these dances.)

Some other types of dancing had a limited following among the nisei. Those accompanied by the songs called *yasuki bushi* were little pantomimes, less formal and stately than the theatrical style. Those accompanied by *ohara bushi* were described as simple round dances. Even in haole ballroom dancing a touch of reversion appeared in 1937. The Hawaiian Japanese Civic Association, following the example of the holoku ball popular among Hawaiians, held a kimono ball. Rich, gay kimonos worn by the girls displayed one of the glories of the old culture. Some of the men, too, wore traditional costume in the somber colors appropriate for them.

The kind of Japanese dance that seemed to attract far the greatest number of nisei was a seasonal one, the *bon* dance. Bon is the Buddhist midsummer festival in honor of the dead, traditionally celebrated about the middle of the seventh month. In Honolulu other bon observances, such as illuminating graves with jade-green lanterns, were followed only by a few; but bon dances were enjoyed by multitudes, any week end in July or August or even early September. Most of them were arranged by the young people's Buddhist associations of various temples. In Honolulu, for several years, beginning in 1929, the custom was exploited by giving a huge public exhibition at one of the athletic fields. Advertisements were put in the newspapers, and haoles as well as Japanese bought tickets. Carefully drilled troupes performed different versions of the dance in competition for prizes contributed by Japanese business firms.

Some of the nisei deplored this commercialization of what was supposedly a religious festival. Yet as John Embree points out in *Japanese Peasant Songs,** these dances may well have antedated Buddhism in Japan. Their association with the festival of the dead seems to be secondary, perhaps depending on coincidence of season, like the use of mistletoe, evergreen, and other pagan trappings at Christmas. One of the attractions of the dance in Japan was opportunity for unsupervised association of young men and women. The tradition seems to have included sexual license. Embree says "Today many of the rural *Bon* dances have been suppressed by the government, while more or less bowdlerized and commercialized forms have been retained in some of the towns and cities." This value, diluted down, could be noted at bon dances in Hawaii, where clusters of young men discussed the charms of the girls as they danced by.

There are many versions of the bon dance, but a common pattern runs through them all. They are given out of doors, at night, and properly by the light of paper lanterns. Musicians are seated in a draped pavilion in the center of the dancing ground. Both men and women dancers wear traditional flowing gowns and wooden

* *Memoirs of the American Folklore Society* (Philadelphia, 1943), Vol. 38.

clogs. Many of the men wrap about their heads towel-like kerchiefs. The dancers form a circle or, if the space is crowded, several circles about the pavilion, and move around it counterclockwise. Through all variations the steps are essentially shuffling retreats and advances in which the clogs are not lifted from the ground, except for an occasional hop in some versions. Gestures of the hands and arms can be summarized as outward and upward swinging motions. In some versions all clap hands together at certain points in the music.

Variants on this pattern still to be seen in Honolulu during the 1930's included some that were considered ancient. The most conspicuous common characteristic of these was the musical accompaniment, which consisted of a solo chant, accompanied by drum and flute. For avowedly modern versions, recently imported from Japan, all the dancers joined in the chorus, and the orchestra was augmented by haole instruments, even saxophones. Hawaiian-born youth ventured a few innovations of their own. Thus, at the public performance in 1934, one recurring Japanese phrase was replaced by "hot-cha-cha," then the height of fashion. The audience was delighted. Another American touch was gum chewing by many of the dancers, who found it dusty work.

The other Japanese holidays most conspicuous in Honolulu were for children, but children so young that the observance showed their parents' interest more than their own. On March 3, an adaptation to the haole calendar of the traditional "third day of the third month," came the girls' festival. It was marked especially by a display of the family dolls, which in the more prosperous families might be numerous and gorgeously dressed. The little guest of honor was supposed to look at the dolls to her heart's content, but not touch them. A public display on the traditional five draped shelves was usually arranged at the Honolulu Academy of Arts.

Far more conspicuous, partly because the display was an out-of-door one, but perhaps also because Japanese culture consistently glorifies the male, was the boys' festival. This came on the fifth day of the fifth month, in Hawaii, May 5. Over the roofs of Japanese houses in which sons had been born during the preceding year floated banners on tall bamboo poles. Some of them were long vertical strips, with the family crest and figures of ancient heroes. Most striking were huge red carp, of cloth or paper, with hoops for mouths. Filled by the wind, they fluttered out over the housetops in realistic imitation of swimming fish. The carp is a symbol of virile fortitude because it is said to swim against the current and to die without a struggle. How much of these displays represented nisei reversion rather than immigrant continuance I found no way to measure. At least they were among the activities about which the generations did not disagree.

Japanese music had adherents among the island born. The daily radio programs formerly given by both Honolulu broadcasting stations are poor evidence of this, for the commercial houses that sponsored them were mainly immigrant controlled, and the music consisted mostly of records imported from Japan. The only special appeal to the nisei in them consisted in the high proportion of modern songs decidedly influenced by the popular American style. A deeper interest was shown by those of the nisei who learned to play Japanese instruments. The most approved instrument for girls was the *koto*, a long zither with 13 strings. The players seat themselves, Japanese fashion, before it. Their motions are graceful and the tone not stranger to haole ears than that of a harpsichord. During the 1930's at least one woman trained in Japan, and several nisei who had learned from their elders, were teachers of this instrument. The koto was sometimes heard in concert with the *shakuhachi,* a bamboo flageolet or longitudinal flute. This seemed to be exclusively a man's instrument. Its tone is pleasant even at first hearing, but the grimaces of the players are distracting to the unaccustomed.

The *samisen* had a social standing rather like that of its distant relative, the banjo, among haoles; that is, not used for serious art but popular for light entertainment. In Honolulu it was heard especially at teahouses. It seemed to be regarded as one of the arts of the geisha, but hardly as a young lady's accomplishment, unless among the Okinawans, by whom it was first introduced to Japan.

Still other Japanese musical styles were not unknown, though rarer. At least one man, Kyoksho Shigemura, was a professional teacher of the *biwa* or Japanese lute, and the tense vocalization with which old narrative songs are performed to its accompaniment. Some of the students of the sword dance learned also the formal chanting that goes with it. So far as I observed, other Japanese instruments like the transverse flute (*fuye*), the Japanese fiddle (*kokyu*), and the little mouth-blown organ (*sho*), were played only by members of the immigrant generation, mainly at Shinto ceremonies or some of the most conservative theatrical performances.

Of the still deeper interest in Japanese music required for composition I found but one example, and this composer's aim was not to carry on a purely Japanese tradi-

tion but to blend it with haole style. This was Allen
Ebesu, trained in European music with emphasis on harmony and composition. Having been born and brought
up in Hawaii, he had also a lifelong familiarity with the
Japanese music heard there. Ebesu's attempt to incorpo-
rate something from both styles in original composition
began with a request from a friend, who had composed
a poem in Japanese, that he set it to music. Early in 1939,
when he had composed two such songs, one of them was
heard in a concert at the Honolulu Academy of Arts.
The conspicuously Japanese characteristic of this song
was a melody mainly pentatonic, some characteristic
progressions, and phrasing influenced by the Japanese
verse form. The harmony was fundamentally European,
though influenced by the Japanese melody. Ebesu was
being encouraged to continue in this vein by Seiki
Tatsumi, European-trained teacher of singing.

An opposite attitude toward the music of their ancestors, one of rather self-conscious deprecation, was
taken by two university students in themes written for
Professor Keesing. One of them wrote (italics my own):
"Japanese music, *if it could be called that,* finds some
adherents among the local winsome entertainers." The
other: "Some Japanese people encourage their children
even to learn Japanese music, koto or samisen, instead of
the piano or violin."

Some nisei girls were skilled in the tea ceremony and
Japanese flower arrangement. In Japan these had been
accomplishments of ladies and gentlemen of leisure. Since
the immigrants were mostly humble, hard-working people, it seems unlikely that any but the few of samurai
rank can have had more than a distant acquaintance with

such graces before coming to Hawaii. But in Honolulu during the 1930's at least three teachers who had studied the tea ceremony in Japan were giving instruction in it. Occasional public demonstrations were given at the Honolulu Academy of Arts. The annual flower shows at the Academy regularly included examples of Japanese flower arrangement. There were several teachers of that, too. Interest in these elegant accomplishments may show, in addition to esthetic reversion, a haolefied tendency to social climbing.

Although more of Japanese architecture than of Chinese was brought to Hawaii by the immigrant generation, less of it has been taken over by the Hawaiian born. One reason for this is probably the difference in time. Comparatively few of the nisei have got along far enough economically to afford building homes of their own. Although they preferred to set up housekeeping for themselves, rented bungalows were the best they could hope for, as a rule. Furniture as well as architecture was likely to be haole; and since wives commonly contributed to the family earnings, haole devices for saving time and labor in housekeeping were in demand. Esthetic reversion was relegated to little decorative objects, but there it did appear: prints, scrolls, porcelain, lacquerware.

Reversion toward Japanese athletics interested only a minority of the nisei; yet the minority was numerous enough to carry on several Japanese sports: sumo wrestling; judo, sporting variant of the old jiujitsu; *kendo*, fencing with bamboo foils; and kyudo, archery. Of these only sumo was a folk sport and really part of the heritage of most of the immigrants. The others were samurai exer-

cises, originally forms of military training; and only the
samurai minority among immigrants was skilled in them.
Accordingly, in the continuance of these sports and reversion to them, the influence of a few leaders has been
conspicuous.

The feeling involved in reversion of this kind seems
best brought out by a sketch of the history of Japanese
athletics in Hawaii, based mainly on an interview with
Dr. Harry I. Kurisaki, one of the pioneers in judo among
the Hawaiian born. The very fact that he knew so much
about it shows an interest like that of "fans" and "dope-
sters" in American sports. A few details, particularly
about fencing and archery, were added by others whose
names are mentioned in the account.

Interest in sumo had its ups and downs, but never died
out entirely. A series of sumo clubs appeared among the
immigrants; most of them short lived, but soon succeeded
by others. At first there were no professional *sumotori*
in the islands; but the prowess of a few of the early
amateurs is still remembered; for one, Kashiwabara,
whose broad-shouldered son Hans grew up to become
a captain of Honolulu police.

About 1910 a troupe of professionals arrived and remained for several years. Three of them settled in Hawaii and one, Kinjo, learned American catch-as-catch-can
wrestling while serving in the American Army, and later
became champion of Hawaii in that style. About 1913
another professional, whose wrestling name was Edosa-
kura or Tokyo-cherry-blossom, was brought from Japan to coach the local amateurs. He married a nisei girl
and eventually went to the island of Maui.

A series of interracial wrestling matches held in Hon-

olulu early in the twentieth century included what may
have been the first public appearance in Hawaii of jiujitsu. At first the Japanese were represented in these con-
tests by a sumo wrestler known professionally as Waka-
minato and considered the strongest Japanese in the
islands. He defeated his first opponent, a Hawaiian, but
was later thrown by an American Negro.

Devotees of Japanese athletics took this defeat as a loss
of face. A deputation went to call on Yajiro Kitayama, an
expert in jiujitsu then living on the island of Hawaii. He
maintained at first that the dignity of this samurai art
would be lowered by public display. But he was finally
convinced that the honor of the Japanese in Hawaii was
at stake. He met the Negro champion and pinned him
with a Japanese arm lock, a hold since adopted in haole
wrestling. Now the spirit of these matches apparently
was not altogether one of sport; and there could hardly
be any rules in a series involving a variety of traditions.
Dr. Kurisaki said that the Negro, mad with pain from
the arm lock, bit Kitayama in the thigh. Thereupon the
jiujitsu expert bore down and broke his opponent's arm.
It was a famous victory, and Kitayama was persuaded
to remain in Honolulu as a coach and instructor in jiujitsu.

Meanwhile judo had been developed in Japan. The
first judo organization in Honolulu was formed in 1908
by Kurisaki and nine of his schoolmates, with Nitaro
Murata as coach. He was an immigrant of samurai family
whose other occupation was bonesetting. In 1910 this
club disbanded when two others, Shobukan and Shinokan,
were formed. Both were still active during the 1930's.
In 1911 the Japanese high school conducted by the Hong-

wanji mission began to teach judo. During the 1930's Reverend Tetsuo Tachibana, in charge of physical education at the school, was the leading expert in Hawaii.

About 1900 the Kobukai, a club for kendo fencing, was organized by Dr. Munikichi Asahina. It had about 20 members. Interest was considerably heightened by the arrival in 1910 of Takashi Wada, whose forefathers had been instructors in fencing to the samurai of Kyushu Island. In his spare time he gave the Honolulu devotees the benefit of his skill. Dr. Asahina was also the pioneer in Japanese archery. In Honolulu this ancient and aristocratic sport was practiced rather fitfully but never altogether forgotten.

These pioneers were of the immigration generation. In 1937 the Buttokai, an athletic organization copied after a Japanese model, was organized for the practice of judo, kendo, and kyudo. By that time active participants were virtually all Hawaiian born. Membership in the three branches was reported as about 800 in Honolulu. Judo devotees were most numerous. Kendo fencers also met regularly at several gymnasiums. The relatively few archers had but one meeting place, on the grounds of a Shinto temple. Their instructors were one of the younger men of the immigrant generation; a priest of the Soto Buddhist mission; and a *kibei*, born in Hawaii but a graduate of a university in Japan.

Sumo, though not so highly organized or taught in schools, seemed to be gaining popularity during the 1930's. The Oahu Sumo Association was organized in 1934 with 300 active members as well as supporting members who were not wrestlers themselves. During 1937 a team of sumo wrestlers from Japanese universities visited

Hawaii and met the island sumotori. Though the visitors won most of their matches, they lost enough to make a contest of it.

All reversion to Japanese culture that involved public display became increasingly uncomfortable from 1939 on, as tension between the United States and Japan increased with the approach of war. What little was left of it by the time the Japanese attacked Pearl Harbor stopped at once then. Whether it will revive, and if so how soon and with what changes, is an interesting question, but with no direct bearing on the present inquiry as to how the nisei had become as American as they were when the war broke out.

On reviewing the evidence of withdrawal from haole dominance, two main points stand out. One is that, while withdrawal has been on the whole a more frequent recourse than aggression, it is still confined to a minority. Withdrawal into psychosis, not investigated here, clearly affects very few. Withdrawal into religion, in any way that greatly changes the life of numbers of people, has been confined to brief movements, most of them limited in area as well as time.

The few cults of local origin that persist, like the Reasonable Service Church, subside into orderly observance of forms not greatly different from those of orthodox Christianity. True, adherence to Buddhism probably involves withdrawal from haole dominance. But it does not prevent conformity to haole culture in other activities. For that matter, Christianity is the religion most prevalent among Hawaiians and island-born Chinese, and appeals to a strong minority among Japanese as well. Fundamentally this too may involve withdrawal. But from the point of view of this inquiry into choice among cultures, adherence to Christianity must be regarded as coöperation with the dominant culture. Finally, any consideration of religion must include the point already made, that agnosticism and indifference are among the commonest attitudes in Hawaii nowadays, particularly among young people, regardless of ancestry. As far as we can judge in a matter where a count of heads is impossible, all forms of religious withdrawal do not add up to anything near a majority. The other salient point is that the kind of withdrawal that seems most prevalent—though still followed only by a minority—is the mildest possible kind, the interest in ancestral art or sport that we have called recreative reversion. This, with the similar finding about aggression, emphasizes another point already suggested —that aggression and withdrawal are proportionate to stress. It is plain that the stress of haole dominance in Hawaii has been mild, as compared to regions that have been swept by native revolts and nativistic religions.

VIII

Coöperation

OF the three main ways to relief from stress, the only one still to be considered is coöperation. This may appear in a variety of forms, corresponding to a wide range of attitudes.

At one extreme is passive conformity, drifting with the current. This is the usual course, probably followed by all of us except where we bring up against some snag. Indeed, life is too short for even the stubbornest of nonconformists to make an issue of more than a few selected points in his behavior. Grading into this, but a little more deliberate, is the attitude of playing safe: "I run the least risk of trouble, and stand the best chance of approval, if I do just as everybody else is doing." Perhaps there are few who do not follow this, too, at some points. Erich Fromm finds it particularly characteristic of democracies, where it constitutes the favorite "Escape from Freedom" for those who have no opinion of their own, or dare not trust what they have. Still rather passive is the resigned sort of coöperation, based on compromise, expressed in the adage "If you can't lick 'em, jine 'em."

Far more active, often indeed excessive, is the coöperation of the ascetic. This has an element of aggression in it. Your ascetic meticulously avoids all that is forbidden, and drives himself to do his full duty. His aggression, so far, is turned in upon himself. It may also be directed against others who do not go so far as he in wringing the last drop of coöperation out of themselves. Any success they win, with their lax ways, is resented. Aggression against them takes the form of anticipating trouble for them, and is often expressed in censorious talk: "Oh yes, they are thriving now. They hold their heads high. But just you wait! Sooner or later they will get what is coming to them."

The extreme of active coöperation is that which the highest American military decoration, the Congressional Medal of Honor, is intended to acknowledge; that is, coöperation carried "above and beyond the call of duty." This, too, involves aggression, as a rule. Insofar as the hero or martyr has to drive himself, the aggression is of the self-punishing ascetic type. Where coöperation itself involves aggression against some enemy, that provides another outlet.

This whole range of coöperative attitudes is represented in Hawaii. Evidence on the subject collected in this study has already been given from another point of view. The chapters on growth of haole prestige showed that all groups considered, except the Oriental immigrants, have come to be mainly haole in their behavior. And even the immigrants have conformed to haole expectation in most of the ways that haoles insist upon. For the rest, deviation in opinion and worship is allowed them under American law. Deviation in little matters that haoles might punish with ridicule is usually kept from public view. And when some of them go so far as to risk punishment by haole police, courts, and jails—by smoking opium, for instance—they keep it as quiet as they can, or perhaps come to some understanding with the police. Haoles themselves do no more. But deviation to that extent is an exception to the rule. The rule among all peoples in Hawaii, as we have seen, is conformity to haole practices.

Another way to phrase this showing is to say that all peoples in Hawaii have, in the main, followed the way of coöperation. So far only passive conformity and playing safe have been considered. Among more active forms of coöperation, the ascetic one has not been explicitly established for Hawaii. It seems not to have been expressed in any mass movement, except in the emphasis on fasting found in the recent Hawaiian cults of the Living God and Reasonable Service, and possibly in the bare feet of devotees of the Filipino cult. (Going barefoot, though, is no hardship in Hawaii. Children of all races do it, except on dress occasions, throughout their school years.)

Only one case has been noted of the extreme kind of asceticism that rejoices in a hair shirt, lies on a couch of spikes, takes long pilgrimages on hands and knees, and so on. That was Reverend Eli Kekipi, who, according to his successor as pastor of the Reasonable Service Church, fasted for 40 days and died six days later. Interpretation of his case would require a penetrating life history. Lack of this kind of data has also prevented identification of less conspicuous individual cases of asceticism. But at least, as far as a casual impression can be trusted, a moderate degree of it seems not uncommon. One of my friends, a part-Hawaiian who has suffered from conduct the opposite of ascetic by some of his relatives, is quietly ascetic in his own principles and conduct. That could be apparent only to those who know him well. But knowing him gives a look of similar asceticism to many of his fellow citizens of all races—faithful performers of humble tasks, meticulous observers of all requirements of correct behavior, often steady churchgoers. They observe all the haole rules; in some cases literally "with a vengeance" in the form of censorious talk.

The classic instance of extreme coöperation, which also had asceticism in it, is the record of nisei from Hawaii in the war. As noted at the beginning of this account, it had wide publicity at the time; and Lind, in *Hawaii's Japanese*, has analyzed it in more detail than would be possible here. Yet a summary seems in order as a picture of this way to relief from stress.

Nisei combat service began with Pearl Harbor. Blake Clark, in one of his magazine articles, reports the promotion of two nisei soldiers for exemplary conduct on this day. Such bravery was not confined to men in uniform. Two nisei civilians at Pearl Harbor saw a machine gunner having difficulty in setting up his gun. They ran to him, helped him steady it, and supplied ammunition. Afterward both needed emergency treatment for burns, presumably from handling the hot gun.

Within a few days another Honolulan, Technical Sergeant Arthur Komori of the regular army, was in the fighting in the Philippines. He served throughout the campaign on Bataan, always keeping one cartridge in his .45 automatic for himself, because, as he later told a reporter for the Honolulu *Star-Bulletin*, "You know what the Japs would have done to me if they caught someone of their own race fighting them on Bataan." Apparently the same thought led his superiors not to leave him with those who finally had to surrender. They had him evacuated to Corregidor and at the last flown to Australia.

Cases like this could not dispel the suspicion which fell upon everybody of Japanese descent in those tense days. Immediately after Pearl Harbor, the R.O.T.C. units of the University of Hawaii and the four Honolulu high schools were mobilized as the Hawaii Territorial Guards. Nisei made up a large part of their membership. The authorities were unwilling at that time to take the risk of disloyalty among them, so the unit was inactivated by an order of January 23, 1942. How the nisei felt about it is indicated by the comment of one of them: "America is our country, but the government won't even let us take a chance on dying for it."

This blow to pride was parried nobly by 125 of the rejected men, mostly from the University of Hawaii. They sent the commanding general a petition, asking to serve in whatever capacity might be assigned them. They were given semimilitary status and assigned to a regiment of engineers. With their numbers later increased to 160, they worked well at a variety of labor jobs. They called themselves the "Varsity Victory Volunteers."

Felt as another blow to pride by some, though not so intended, was the shipment to the American mainland in June, 1942, of a provisional battalion of nisei, made up of former members of the 298th and 299th Infantry, Hawaii National Guard. Under the Selective Service Act they had been called to active duty before Pearl Harbor. Actually the decision to move them was intended as an honor, a chance to prove themselves; and a good many of them so understood it. Yet the difficulty of using them in the Pacific, with perhaps some doubt as to their feeling toward Japan, did presumably enter into the decision.

And that was the side which first impressed some of the Japanese community, among whom American opinion of them was naturally a very tender subject in those days. Why were only the Japanese taken? A rumor got around that they were to be interned. To dispel this, the army announced that they were to be trained for combat duty, though not in the Pacific. They formed the 100th Infantry Battalion.

In January, 1943, as another recognition of good behavior, volunteering was thrown open to a limited number of nisei from Hawaii. The quota at first was 1,500. The number of volunteers in the first two weeks of registration was 7,425. The quota was raised to 2,600. The number of volunteers rose to 9,507. Nearly 3,000 sailed early in April, to be trained on the mainland as the 442d Regimental Combat Team.

The 100th Infantry Battalion landed at Anzio, and first met the enemy in the hills above Salerno in September, 1943. In a War Department release of October 21 Captain Taro Suzuki, who commanded the first company under fire, described that experience:

Our leading scouts rounded a bend and three German machine guns opened up. There was nothing to do but go to work on them alone because nobody to the rear could see to fire the heavy stuff. One platoon went out to the right, one straight ahead, and a squad went off to the left. Trouble was, every time a man would stick his head up to take a look, machine gun bullets cut right close by.

As if we didn't have trouble enough, the Germans broke everything loose on us—machine guns, mortars, rifles and heavy artillery. Back where our support was they could see the smoke from the big guns the Germans were firing at us, but it didn't do us any good. They didn't know where we were so didn't dare fire. Finally, we spotted orange flashes. They were only pinpoints and lasted a split second, but it was enough to show they were guns firing.

You know what stopped all that Nazi wrath? Our little 60 mm. mortars. We got them on there and they went right in. Boy, it felt good to see them dropping! The machine gunners pulled out after the big guns quit and our riflemen started making rapid headway on them.

The 100th Battalion is credited with taking San Michele in a night attack and launching the first infantry assault around Cassino. On the day when the account just quoted was released, Private First Class Thomas I. Yamanaga of Honolulu was killed in action. He was posthumously awarded the Distinguished Service Cross. His citation follows:

"The company in which he was a gunner was pinned down by heavy machine gun fire from the front in October in Italy. On his own initiative he worked his way forward in full view of the enemy to a position where he could engage an enemy gun with his automatic rifle. He immediately delivered such effective fire that the enemy gun was silenced, whereupon his company was no longer pinned down and successfully continued the attack. He was mortally wounded in rendering this outstanding service to his fellow soldiers." Yamanaga's heroism is only one case of many.

In July, 1944, it was announced that the 442d Regimental Combat Team was in action in Italy, taking part with the Fifth Army in the advance toward Livorno. The veteran 100th Battalion now formed part of this larger nisei unit.

In October, 1944, the 442d appeared in France. It took a leading part in opening the way through the Vosges mountains to Strasbourg. It was the first to reach a "lost battalion" cut off in the forests for a week. In the spring of 1945 it returned to Italy. The regiment suffered total casualties of 9,230, three times its original battle strength. Only six members were absent without leave. Every one of them escaped from a hospital to return to combat. It seems to have become a tradition with them. The regiment won six Distinguished Unit citations, and was chosen to lead the victory march at Livorno. It has been called "probably the most decorated unit in United States military history."

Although 172 of the 442d applied for combat duty against Japan, only a few nisei from Hawaii were actually assigned to the Pacific. Most of them served as interpreters. Some of these, too, risked their lives. On Okinawa, Interpreter Lieutenant Wallace S. Amioka of Honolulu accompanied a patrol searching for guerrillas who had hid out after the capture of the island. When they came upon the highest ranking officer of the guerrillas, it was Amioka's duty to take the risk of approaching and trying to persuade him to surrender. Incidentally, this mission did not succeed; the officer was killed in trying to escape.

Blake Clark gives a more spectacular example: "On Saipan, Sgt. Koichi Kubo volunteered to be lowered by rope down a cliff to a cave where starving Saipan natives crouched in fear for five days, refusing American pleas to accept aid. Unarmed and ignoring a Jap rifle at his back, Kubo calmly reasoned with them. Soon after he had climbed back up the cliff, the whole assembly straggled in. Kubo was decorated with the Bronze Star for his daring mission."

There seems to be no room for doubt that this record represents something beyond the ordinary. These men responded to extreme stress by extreme coöperation.

IX

Beyond Hawaii

RELATIONSHIPS among the different peoples in Hawaii have gone along, not perfectly, yet exceptionally well. Is it because people there are wiser or kinder than others? Hardly, although the people of Hawaii, with a record like this, cannot be deficient in wisdom or kindness. What then can Hawaii offer, by way of a prescription for good will among men? There are so many places in the world now where people of American or European heritage have put themselves in charge of populations alien to them, that any example of success in such an undertaking, even moderate success, should be a great help.

First, a review of the main findings. A variety of factors, among which haole technological superiority may have been the most important, gradually established haole prestige among Hawaiians. Most of the Oriental immigrants resisted haole prestige—at least before Pearl Harbor. But their Hawaiian-born children accepted it wholeheartedly.

Haole dominance, once established, subjected all non-haoles to stress, but this was mild as compared with places where relationships among different peoples have been less friendly. Of the three main ways to relief from stress, the desperate one of aggression has not predominated unless among Hawaiians at two periods of maximum stress —one about the 1830's, when the haoles were rapidly assuming economic and religious dominance; the other in the 1880's and 1890's, when haoles were progressively taking over the government. (Aggression, some of it in the form of suicide, seems also to have been rather frequent among Chinese for a brief period, in response to haole opposition to them.) Among both Hawaiians and Orientals, the only form of aggression that has been at all common recently is the mildest possible one—the verbal form of grumbling.

The more extreme forms of withdrawal, into happy-go-lucky apathy and into religious ecstasy, seem also to have been more frequent among Hawaiians than Orientals. This corresponds to greater stress imposed upon the Hawaiians. As lords of the land before the others arrived, they had the most to lose in descending to a subordinate position. Besides, the disparity between their culture and that of the haoles was greater than in the case of the Orientals. This added to the special stress imposed upon them in adapting to a new, haole dispensation.

Recreative reversion, the mildest form of withdrawal, seems to have been gaining ground during the last generation over more pronounced forms.

Coöperation has been the dominant response among all peoples for a generation or more.

This showing suggests in the first place that the present superiority in technology of Euro-American (haole) culture is enough under most circumstances to ensure the prestige of heirs to that culture without artificial aids. The white man does not have to dress for dinner and wear a coat in the hot sun in order to hold his prestige. He does not have to require the other kind of man to go around to the back door, take off his hat, address the white man with respectful formality, and smilingly accept condescending familiarity in return. The culture of the white man, however far from being a royal road to happiness, has enough advantages to win respect on its merits. All he has to do to gain prestige is show, without ostentation, what he can accomplish. (That does include accomplishment of one kind we may deplore, military skill in destroying an enemy, as well as of kinds we admire, such as improvement of health.)

Hawaii's experience suggests further that invidious devices like segregation and codes of subservience are not only unnecessary but positively harmful. The milder the stress, the more coöperative the response. An apparent exception to this, the extreme coöperation of the nisei soldiers in response to the heavy stress imposed upon them, can be attributed to two factors. In the first place, a coöperative response was already solidly established among them. In the second place, after the early months of frustration and rebuff, the opportunity of coöperation was opened to them and urged upon them.

Comparison with other regions should test these conclusions. To take one example, the Japanese immigrants and nisei of the Pacific Coast states were subjected to much severer stress than those of Hawaii, by being deprived of their homes and means of livelihood and segregated in relocation centers. Accordingly, forms of aggression quite unlike anything in Hawaii appeared among them: strikes, riots, and declarations, even on the part of nisei, of allegiance to Japan. Coöperative responses among them were correspondingly less frequent. Lind points out in *Hawaii's Japanese* that "the number of enlistments in Hawaii was over nine times that in continental United

States, although the number of draftable nisei in the two areas was roughly the same."

The policy indicated for rulers of alien peoples is to keep the stress of contact as mild as they can. One way to do this is to order changes only when, after fullest possible consideration of their probable consequences, they seem necessary; and then to put them into effect as gradually, and as politely, as possible. Change imposes stress; and the greater and more abrupt the change, the severer the stress.

Stress cannot be eliminated. Indeed, given human fallibility, a certain amount of unnecessary, unreasonable stress must be expected. The evidence from Hawaii suggests promising ways of dealing with it, in terms of the three main ways to relief:

1. *Coöperation.* Fullest opportunity should be allowed for this most desirable of responses. The point was admirably expressed, before Pearl Harbor, by Major John Otto, then in charge of the Reserve Officers' Training unit at the University of Hawaii. He said of his nisei students, "These boys are as American as we let them be." Time showed he was right. As far as government is concerned, this would involve leaving the administration of local affairs as far as possible to the people themselves, and as far as possible through their traditional agencies, however bizarre these may seem to the foreign ruler.

2. *Withdrawal.* All forms of withdrawal not unmistakably harmful should be permitted as ways of relief from stress. Harmless forms like recreative reversion, which do not prevent coöperation in essentials, should be encouraged, if this can be done without damping their spontaneity. Even harmful forms, such as hysterical reli-

gious cults, may burn out more quickly if left to themselves. The cult of the sacred stones of Wahiawa, for example (not particularly harmful from an administrator's point of view) subsided rather quickly without official opposition.

3. *Aggression.* As long as it takes the ascetic form, whereby coöperation is intensified, even aggression can be most useful. In another form, that of grumbling, it may have several uses. First, as an outlet for tension. Second, as a source of criticism that may involve valuable suggestions. Third, as a warning that stress is becoming too severe.

Any ruler must of course suppress overt aggression—rebellion—against his own authority. But that is itself a symptom of failure. Unless the stress imposed has been so extreme as to drive its victims to desperation, overt aggression can probably be discouraged by a next-to-last resort—a show of force which makes it plain that aggression would have little chance of success.

Bibliography

ONLY works which have contributed specifically to this study are listed. Fuller bibliographies appear elsewhere; particularly that on native Hawaiian culture in An Introduction to Polynesian Anthropology by Te Rangi Hiroa (Peter H. Buck), B. P. Bishop Museum, Bull. 187, Honolulu. A general classification by subject matter has been attempted for the sake of convenience. Works which contain material on more than one of the categories are listed under the one that seems predominant.

General Description

BATES, GEORGE W. ("A Haole"), Sandwich Island Notes. New York, Harper, 1854.

BEECHEY, F. W., Narrative of a Voyage to the Pacific . . . . London, H. Colburn and R. Bentley, 1831.

BRIGGS, LLOYD VERNON, Experiences of a Medical Student in Honolulu . . . . 1881. Boston, David D. Nickerson Company, 1926.

CAMPBELL, ARCHIBALD, A Voyage around the World from 1806 to 1812 . . . with an account of the present state of the Sandwich Islands . . . . Edinburgh, A. Constable & Co., 1816.

CLEMENS, SAMUEL L. (Mark Twain), Letters from the Sandwich Islands. San Francisco, The Grabhorn Press, 1937.

——— Roughing It. Hartford, American Publishing Company, 1872.

CLEVELAND, RICHARD J., A Narrative of Voyages and Commercial Enterprises. 2d ed. Cambridge, J. Owen, 1843. 2 vols.

COOK, JAMES, A Voyage to the Pacific Ocean, 1776–1780. London, G. Nicol and T. Cadell, 1785. 2 vols. (Continued after Cook's death by James King, *q.v.*)

FREYCINET, LOUIS DE, Voyage autour du monde . . . pendant les années 1817–1820. Paris, Imprimerie Royale, 1829.

GEROULD, KATHERINE FULLERTON, Hawaii: Scenes and Impressions. New York, C. Scribner's Sons, 1916.

GESSLER, CLIFFORD, HAWAII: Isles of Enchantment. New York, D. Appleton–Century Company, 1937.

GOLOVNIN, CAPTAIN, Golovnin's Visit to Hawaii in 1818, trans. from the Russian of A Tour around the World, by Joseph Barth, *The Friend*, 52: 50–53, 60–62.

HILL, S. S., Travels in the Sandwich and Society Islands. London, Chapman and Hall, 1856.

KING, JAMES A., A Voyage to the Pacific Ocean, Vol. 3. London, G. Nicol and T. Cadell, 1785. (A continuation of Captain Cook's narrative, listed above.)

KOTZEBUE, OTTO VON, A Voyage of Discovery into the South Sea . . . in the Years 1815–1818. English trans. London, Longman, Hurst, Rees, Orme, and Brown, 1821. 3 vols.

LISIANSKY, UREY, A Voyage round the World in the Years 1803–1806. London, printed for J. Booth, 1814.

LYMAN, CHESTER S., Around the Horn to the Sandwich Islands and California, 1845–1850. New Haven, Yale University Press, 1924. (An abridgement of Lyman's Journal.) The complete ms. and a typed copy are in the Hawaiian Mission Children's Assn. Library, Honolulu.

MENZIES, Archibald, Hawaii Nei 128 Years Ago. Honolulu [W. F. Wilson], 1920. (From the journal of Vancouver's naturalist and physician.)

PARKE, WILLIAM C., Personal Reminiscences of William C. Parke, Marshal of the Hawaiian Islands from 1850 to

1884. Cambridge (Mass.) printed at the University Press, 1897.

PORTEUS, STANLEY D., Calabashes and Kings, an Introduction to Hawaii. Palo Alto, Pacific Books, 1945.

PORTLOCK, NATHANIEL, A Voyage round the World . . . . London, printed for Stockdale, and G. Goulding, 1789.

STEVENSON, ROBERT LOUIS, Letters and Miscellanies . . . . New York, C. Scribner, 1918.

STODDARD, CHARLES WARREN, Hawaiian Life. Chicago and New York, F. T. Neely, 1894.

TAYLOR, CHARLES M., Vacation Days in Hawaii and Japan. Philadelphia, G. W. Jacobs & Co., 1898.

TURNBULL, JOHN, A Voyage round the World, in the Years 1800 . . . 1804. 2d ed. London, A. Maxwell, 1813.

VANCOUVER, GEORGE, A Voyage of Discovery to the North Pacific Ocean . . . . London, printed for J. Stockdale, 1801.

WILKES, CHARLES, Narrative of the U. S. Exploring Expedition . . . . Philadelphia, Lea and Blanchard, 1845. 5 vols.

WITHINGTON, ANTOINETTE, Hawaiian Tapestry. New York, Harper & Brothers, 1937.

Missionaries

AMERICAN BOARD OF COMMISSIONERS FOR FOREIGN MISSIONS, First Ten Annual Reports . . . . Boston, 1834.

——— Prudential Committee. Instructions of the Prudential Committee . . . to the Sandwich Islands Mission. Lahainaluna, Press of the Mission Seminary, 1838.

ANDERSON, RUFUS, The Hawaiian Islands, Their Progress and Condition under Missionary Labors. New York, Sheldon & Co. 1864.

Answers by the Sandwich Islands missionaries to the questions in the circular of March 15, 1833, sent to missionaries of the American Board . . . . Ms. in Hawaiian Mission Children's Assn. Library, Honolulu.

Answers to questions proposed by His Excellency B. C. Wyllie, and addressed to all the missionaries in the Hawaiian Islands. Honolulu, n.p., 1848.

BINGHAM, HIRAM, A Residence of 21 Years in the Sandwich Islands. Hartford, H. Huntington, 1847.

BISHOP, SERENO E., Reminiscences of Old Hawaii. Honolulu, Hawaiian Gazette Company Ltd., 1916.

DAMON, S. C., Letters from Polynesia, No. IV. *Sailors' Magazine*, November, 1852. (In Hawaiiana, bound collection of miscellaneous periodicals in the Hawaii Mission Children's Assn. Library, Honolulu.)

DWIGHT, REVEREND E. W., Memoirs of Obookiah . . . . Elizabethtown, N. J., published by Edson Hart, J. and E. Sanderson, printers, 1819.

GOWEN, H. H., The Paradise of the Pacific. London, Skeffington & Son, 1892.

GULICK, REVEREND and MRS. ORRAMEL. The Pilgrims of Hawaii . . . . New York and London, Fleming H. Revell Company, 1918.

HAWAIIAN MISSION CENTENNIAL, The Centennial Book, 100 Years of Christian Civilization in Hawaii. Honolulu, n.p., 1920.

JUDD, LAURA FISH, Honolulu, Sketches of Life . . . from 1828 to 1861. New York, A. D. F. Randolph & Co., 1880.

LYMAN, HENRY MUNSON, Hawaiian Yesterdays. Chicago, A. C. McClurg & Co., 1906.

MISSIONARY LETTERS, 8 vols., in Hawaiian Mission Children's Assn. Library. Originals in files of the American Board, Boston.

RESTARICK, HENRY B. Hawaii, 1778–1920, from the Viewpoint of a Bishop. Honolulu, Paradise of the Pacific, 1924.

RICHARDS, MARY ATHERTON, The Chiefs' Children's School, a Record Compiled from the Diary and Letters of Amos

Starr Cooke and Juliet Montague Cooke. Honolulu, Honolulu Star-Bulletin, 1937.

STEWART, C. S., A Residence in the Sandwich Islands. 5th ed. Boston, Weeks, Jordan & Co., 1839.

The Liquor Traffic in the Hawaiian Islands from 1870 to 1895. Prepared for the Y.M.C.A. Honolulu, n.d.

THURSTON, MRS. LUCY G., Life and Times . . . Gathered from Letters and Journals. Ann Arbor, 1832. 3d ed. Honolulu, 1934.

YZENDOORN, REGINALD, History of the Catholic Mission in the Hawaiian Islands. Honolulu Star-Bulletin, Honolulu, 1927.

History and Social Science

ADAMS, ROMANZO, Interracial Marriage in Hawaii. New York, Macmillan Company, 1937.

────── The Peoples of Hawaii. Honolulu, American Council, Institute of Pacific Relations, 1933.

────── The Unorthodox Race Doctrine of Hawaii; in American Sociological Society, Race and Culture Contacts. New York and London, McGraw-Hill, 1934.

ALEXANDER, W. D., A Brief History of the Hawaiian People. New York, American Book Company, 1899.

────── A Statement of Facts Relating to Politics during Kalakaua's Reign: Report of the Committee on Foreign Relations, U. S. Senate, 53d Congress, 2d session, Vol. 2, pp. 1453–1471. Government Printing Office, Washington, 1894.

ANDREWS, LORRIN, A Dictionary of the Hawaiian Language. Revised by Henry H. Parker. Honolulu, Board of Commissioners of Public Archives of the Territory of Hawaii, 1922.

BEAGLEHOLE, ERNEST, Some Modern Hawaiians. University of Hawaii, Research Publication No. 19. Honolulu, University of Hawaii, 1937.

BECKWITH, MARTHA W. (ed.), Kepelino's Traditions of Hawaii. B. P. Bishop Museum, Bull. 95. Honolulu, 1932.

BICKNELL, JAMES, Hoomanamana—Idolatry. Honolulu, n.d., n.p.

BLACKMAN, W. F., The Making of Hawaii. New York, Macmillan Company, 1906.

Blount's Report on Annexation of Hawaii; in President's Message Relating to the Hawaiian Islands, House Executive Documents, 53d Congress, No. 47. Washington, 1895.

BRADLEY, HAROLD WHITMAN, The American Frontier in Hawaii, Stanford University, Stanford University Press, 1942.

COBB, JOHN N., Commercial Fisheries; in Jordan, David S., and Evermann, Barton W., The Aquatic Resources of the Hawaiian Islands. U. S. Fish Commission, Bull. for 1903. Washington, Government Printing Office, 1905.

Coulter, John W., Land Utilization in the Hawaiian Islands. University of Hawaii, Research Publication No. 8. Honolulu, University of Hawaii, 1933.

—— Population and Utilization of Land and Sea in Hawaii, 1853. B. P. Bishop Museum, Bull. 88. Honolulu, 1931.

DAHLGREN, E. W., Were the Hawaiians Visited by the Spaniards before Their Discovery by Captain Cook in 1778? Kungl. Svenska Vetenskapsakademiens Handlung, Band 57, No. 4. Stockholm, 1916.

DIBBLE, SHELDON, A History of the Sandwich Islands. Reprint of 1843 ed. Honolulu, T. G. Thrum, 1909.

ELLIS, WILLIAM, Polynesian Researches. New York, J. and J. Harper, 1833. 4 vols. (Vol. 4 also reprinted from London 1827 ed. as A Narrative of a Tour through Hawaii, Honolulu, Hawaiian Gazette Company, 1917.)

EMERSON, N. B., Causes of Decline of Ancient Hawaiian Sports, *The Friend*, 1892.

—— Unwritten Literature of Hawaii. Smithsonian Institution, Bureau of American Ethnology, Bull. 38. Washington, Government Printing Office, 1909.

FORNANDER, ABRAHAM, An Account of the Polynesian Race. London, Trübner & Co., 1878–1885. 3 vols.

—— Fornander Collection of Hawaiian Antiquities and Folklore. B. P. Bishop Museum, Memoirs, Vols. 4, 5, and 6. Honolulu, 1916–1920.

GIBSON, WALTER MURRAY. Sanitary Instructions for Hawaiians. Honolulu, printed by P. C. Advertiser Company, 1880.

GLICK, CLARENCE, The Relation between Position and Status in the Assimilation of Chinese in Hawaii, *American Journal of Sociology*, Vol. 47, No. 5, 1942.

HAMAMOTO, H., The Fishing Industry of Hawaii, a thesis for the degree of Bachelor of Arts, No. 10, 1928. University of Hawaii.

HANDY, E. S. C., Cultural Revolution in Hawaii. Honolulu, Institute of Pacific Relations, 1931.

—— and Pukui, Mary K., Ohana, the Dispersed Community of Kanaka. Honolulu, Institute of Pacific Relations, 1935.

Hawaii Board of Health, Kingdom of Hawaii, and Board of Health, Territory of Hawaii, Annual Reports.

Hawaii Territorial Governor, Territory of Hawaii, Annual Reports.

HEEN, ELIZABETH L., The Hawaiians of Papakolea, a thesis for the degree of Master of Arts, 1936. Ms. in University of Hawaii Library.

HOBBS, JEAN, Hawaii: a Pageant of the Soil. Palo Alto, Stanford University Press, 1935.

JARVES, JAMES J., History of the Hawaiian or Sandwich Islands. Boston, Tappan and Dennet, 1843.

JONES, STELLA M., Economic Adjustment of Hawaiians to European Culture, *Pacific Affairs*, Vol. 4, No. 11, 1931.

JUDD, BERNICE, Voyages to Hawaii before 1860. Honolulu, Hawaiian Mission Children's Society, 1929.

KEESING, FELIX M., Hawaiian Homesteading on Molokai. University of Hawaii, Research Publication No. 12. Honolulu, 1936.

KENN, CHARLES W., I Am a Hawaiian, *Paradise of the Pacific*, Vol. 48, No. 11, 1936.

KONISHI, O. K., Fishing Industry of Hawaii. Reports of Students in Economics and Business, No. 6, 1930. University of Hawaii.

KUYKENDALL, RALPH S., The Hawaiian Kingdom, 1778–1854. Honolulu, University of Hawaii, 1938.

LIND, ANDREW W., An Island Community: Ecological Succession in Hawaii. Chicago, University of Chicago Press, 1938.

――― Modifications of Hawaiian Character; in American Sociological Society, Race and Culture Contacts. New York and London, McGraw-Hill, 1934.

――― Occupational Attitudes of Orientals in Hawaii, *Sociology and Social Research*, Vol. 12, No. 3, 1929.

――― Occupational Trends among Immigrant Groups in Hawaii, *Social Forces*, Vol. 7, No. 2, 1928.

LORDEN, DORIS M., The Chinese-Hawaiian Family, *American Journal of Sociology*, Vol. 40, No. 4, 1935.

MALO, DAVID, Hawaiian Antiquities. Honolulu, Hawaiian Gazette Company, 1903.

PRATT, JULIUS W., Expansionists of 1898, the Acquisition of Hawaii and the Spanish Islands. Baltimore, Johns Hopkins Press, 1936.

REINECKE, JOHN E., Language and Dialect in Hawaii, a thesis for the degree of Master of Arts, 1935. University of Hawaii.

Royal Hawaiian Agricultural Society, Transactions, Vol. 1, 1850–1856.

SMITH, W. C., Americans in Process, a Study of Our Citizens

of Oriental Ancestry. Ann Arbor, Edwards Brothers, 1937.

Sociology Club, University of Hawaii, Social Process in Hawaii. Honolulu, Annual since 1935. (Articles by faculty members and students.)

STOKES, JOHN F. G., Iron with the Early Hawaiians. Hawaiian Historical Society, Papers, No. 18, Honolulu, 1931.

YOUNG, LUCIEN, The Boston at Hawaii. Washington, Gibson Brothers, 1898.

Chinese in Hawaii

AUSTIN, J., THURSTON, L. A., DAMON, S. M., and ASHFORD, C. W., Reply of the Cabinet to the Petition of the Citizens of Honolulu Regarding Chinese Restriction. Honolulu, n.p., 1889. Also included in Biennial Report of the Board of Immigration to the Legislature, Session of 1890.

Chinese of Hawaii, The (A "Who's Who" with special articles). Honolulu, Overseas Penman Club, 1929 and 1936.

Chinese Supplement, *The Friend*. Containing Tours among the Chinese by F. W. Damon, The Chinese in Hawaii by J. A. Cruzan, etc. In quarterly installments, 1882.

COULTER, J. W., and CHUN, C. K., Chinese Rice Farmers in Hawaii. University of Hawaii, Research Publication No. 16, 1937.

GIRVIN, JAMES W., Articles on Chinese in Hawaii, *Pacific Commercial Advertiser*, July 6, 1901, January 1, 1902, September 5, 1903, July 2, 1906.

HSIEH T'ING-YU, The Chinese in Hawaii, *Chinese Social and Political Science Review*, Vol. 14, 1930.

LAM, FRED K., A Survey of the Chinese in Hawaii, *Mid-Pacific Magazine*, Vol. 38, No. 6, 1929.

Marshal of the Hawaiian Kingdom, Disclosures as to the Chinese Secret Societies, Honolulu, n.p., 1884.

OLESON, W. B., Our Chinese Invasion, *The Friend*, 1887.

REUTER, E. B., The Social Process with Special Reference to Patterns of Personality among the Chinese in Hawaii. Sociological Society of America, Publications, Vol. 26, No. 3, 1932.

SCOTT, WINIFRED ALLEN, The Chinese Theater in Honolulu, *Paradise of the Pacific*, Vol. 42, No. 5, 1929.

(General works, especially Social Process in Hawaii, also contain valuable material.)

Japanese in Hawaii

BOUSLOG, CHARLES S., Hawaii Shows Japan and Asia, *Asia and the Americas*, February, 1943.

CLARK, BLAKE, Remember Pearl Harbor. Toronto, McLeod, 1942. Also the following articles on the nisei in World War II: Never Shoot a Hawaiian More than Twice, *Reader's Digest*, December, 1942; Some Japanese in Hawaii, *Asia and the Americas*, December, 1942; The Japanese in Hawaii, *New Republic*, September 14, 1942.

CLARK, BLAKE, and RUSSELL, OLAND D., Japanese-American Soldiers Make Good, *American Mercury*, June, 1945, and *Reader's Digest*, July, 1945.

Emergency Service Committee, Report. Honolulu, 1944.

HARADA, TASUKU, The Social Status of the Japanese in Hawaii. Honolulu, Institute of Pacific Relations, 1927.

Hawaiian Japanese Annual and Directory, Honolulu, Nippu Jiji Publishing Company, 1933.

HOBSON, THOMAS C., Japan's "Peaceful Invasion": Hawaiian Almanac and Annual, 1898.

Honolulu *Star-Bulletin*, Golden Jubilee Section: A tribute to the Japanese Who Arrived in Hawaii 50 Years Ago. February 16, 1935.

IMAMURA, Y., A Short History of the Hongwanji Buddhist Mission in Hawaii. Honolulu, Publishing Bureau of Hongwanji Buddhist Mission, 1927.

INOUYE, SOUNO, Articles in Honolulu *Advertiser*, 1927–1930.

LIND, ANDREW W., Hawaii's Japanese: an Experiment in Democracy. Princeton, Princeton University Press, 1946.

MASUOKA, JITSUISHI, Race Attitudes of the Japanese People in Hawaii, a thesis for the degree of Master of Arts in sociology, 1931. Ms. in University of Hawaii Library.

SCUDDER, DOREMUS, Hawaii's Experience with the Japanese. Annals of the American Academy of Political and Social Science, Vol. 93, No. 182, 1921.

SHEBA, S., Japanese Home Life in Honolulu, *Mid-Pacific Magazine*, Vol. 1, 1911.

TAJIMA, PAUL J., Japanese Buddhism in Hawaii, a thesis for the degree of Master of Arts, 1935. Ms. in University of Hawaii Library.

TERRY, JOHN, With Hawaii's AJA boys at Camp Shelby. Reprinted by Honolulu *Star-Bulletin* from a series of articles. Honolulu, Honolulu Star-Bulletin (ca. 1943).

WAKUKAWA, ERNEST K., A History of the Japanese People in Hawaii. Honolulu, Toyoshoin, 1938.

War Department, Bureau of Public Relations. Press releases on nisei from Hawaii in World War II; especially January 28, 1943; October 21, 1943.

(Also general works, particularly Social Process in Hawaii.)

Periodicals

Bulletin (daily), Honolulu, 1882–1912.

Friend, The (monthly), Honolulu, 1843—.

Hawaiian Almanac and Annual ("Thrum's Annual"), 1875—.

Honolulu *Advertiser* (daily), 1882—.

Honolulu *Star-Bulletin* (daily), 1912—.

Mid-Pacific Magazine (monthly), 1911–1936.

Missionary Herald (monthly), 1821–1907. (Contains extracts from the journal of the mission begun aboard the brig *Thaddeus* in 1820. The complete journal is in the files of the American Board in Boston, and a typed copy at the Hawaiian Mission Children's Assn. Library in Honolulu.)

Pacific Commercial Advertiser (weekly), 1856–1888.

Paradise of the Pacific (monthly), 1888—.

Polynesian, The (weekly), 1840–1841, 1844–1863.

Index